Daily grace

The Gospel according to Mark

by George M. Philip

 EVANGELICAL PRESS

RUTHERFORD HOUSE

Encouraging Effective Ministry

EVANGELICAL PRESS
Faverdale North Industrial Estate, Darlington DL3 0PH,
England

Evangelical Press USA
P. O. Box 84, Auburn, MA 01501, USA

e-mail: sales@evangelicalpress.org

web: http://www.evangelicalpress.org

RUTHERFORD HOUSE
17 Claremont Park, Edinburgh EH6 7PJ,
Scotland

First published 2001

British Library Cataloguing in Publication Data available

ISBN 0 85234 468 6

Printed and bound in Great Britain by Creative Print &
Design, Ebbw Vale, Wales.

To
The Sandyford Record Team
without whose dedication the original Notes could not have appeared.

Introduction

The habit of reading some verses of the Bible each day is a good and wise one. If we do this with the Gospel according to Mark we will in fact keep company with Jesus and hear his words. Mark's account of the life of Jesus is the simplest and shortest of the four Gospel records, incident after incident being described with the repeated use of the word 'immediately'. It is generally accepted that this was the first of the Gospels to be written down, probably within the period A. D. 40-65. We cannot be dogmatic but it seems that 1 and 2 Thessalonians and Galatians were already written and in circulation before this Gospel. It is clear from Acts 10:36-43 that among the first generation Christians the stories of Jesus were well known and were being passed on orally, but the time came when it was necessary for the accurate preservation of the facts that the story should be compiled and written down. It is believed that Mark's Gospel was written in Rome, where Mark was in close touch with Peter who provided him with much of the material (1 Peter 5:13). It may well be that the young man who ran away in Gethsemane was Mark himself (Mark 14:51) and that the house referred to in Mark 14:14-15 was Mark's home. Mark was the cousin of Barnabas (Colossians 4:10); he had been on Paul's missionary team for a time and then contracted out (Acts 15:36-40); later he was restored and became a man of great spiritual worth to Paul when he faced trial and death (2 Tim. 4: 11). In Acts 12:12 we are told that the church met in Mark's mother's house and in Philemon

24 Mark is spoken of as one of Paul's fellow-workers. All in all, this young man seems to have been an ideal person to record the story of Jesus and, if he obtained details from Peter, we can be sure they were vivid, well remembered, and passed on with a throb of urgency.

The story begins

Read also John 1:1-14

Mark plunges right into his theme, which is the gospel, the good news, or the 'God-news' of or about Jesus Christ, whom he immediately identifies as the Son of God. The emphasis is not on a message or a system of teaching, but on a person, Jesus Christ: who he is and what he did. Mark does not begin his story in Bethlehem as Matthew and Luke do: Matthew, with the Jews in mind, traces the story back to Abraham; while Luke, writing for Gentiles, goes back to Adam and Eve (Matt. 1:1-17; Luke 3:23-38). John begins his story in the realms of eternity and speaks of the eternal Word being made flesh (John 1:1-14). Mark was in no doubt that Jesus is the Christ, the Son of the living God (Mark 9:2-7; 14:61-62; Matt. 16:13-17), sent by God into the world 'when the fulness of the time was come' (Gal. 4:4, AV). For Mark the beginning of all the good news is found in God. It was God who took the initiative. It was God who broke into the human situation, in the person of his Son. It was God who sent his Son to be the Saviour of the world (1 John 4:14). The central affirmation of the gospel is that Jesus Christ came into the world to save sinners (1 Tim. 1:15). He broke into the world of religion (at its best and at its lowest) and declared that religion — which has all to do with man seeking to reach God, find God and please God by his own efforts — cannot bring salvation. Religion is about man reaching up to God, whereas the gospel is all about God reaching down and coming to this earth in his Son. Jesus said the Son of Man came to seek and to save that which is lost (Luke 19:10).

The promised Saviour

Read also Isaiah 40:1-9

The appearance of Jesus Christ on the world stage should not have been unexpected, because it was promised in the Old Testament and prepared for down the generations of history. To emphasize this theme of God's careful preparation and his promise to send a messenger to prepare for the 'crisis' day, Mark brings together Old Testament quotations, referring to Isaiah but quoting first from Malachi (Mal. 3:1; Isa. 40:3; and possibly Isa. 40:9; Exod. 23:20). He directs attention to the ministry of John the Baptist to emphasize that this was the man, raised by God, to prepare the people for the coming of God's promised Saviour. That we should always be prepared in readiness for God to act decisively in history is a challenge to believers in every generation. We pray for God to work mightily. We pray for revival. But are we ready? If a whole city was suddenly convicted of sin and constrained by the Holy Spirit to crowd into churches and other places to seek salvation, would we be ready? Would we be aware of the stirring of such activity of God or would we be taken by surprise? Would we have to ask God to excuse us from involvement because our diaries were filled with previous engagements? God may well work where he is not expected, not in a recognized 'Jerusalem' but 'in the wilderness'. Mark's main emphasis here is that the gospel is not an emergency measure, not a desperate last-minute attempt by God to retrieve something from a broken-down world, but a clear, decisive, well-prepared plan of action to deal with sin and to destroy the works of the devil (Heb. 9:26; 1 John 3:8). It is indeed a glorious gospel!

The forerunner

Read also Luke 1:1-17

The gospel begins with God the Father, who sent his Son into a prepared situation; God the Son, who came as the Lamb of God to take away the sin of the world (John 1:29, 36); and God the Spirit, whose power convicts, converts and enables with newness of life (v. 8). What was planned in eternity was about to appear in history. John came; and both his birth and his ministry were a vital part of God's overall plan, as Luke 1:8-17 makes plain. His ministry began and carried with it such unction from God that the whole community was stirred. By word of mouth, not by a vast publicity programme, the news spread, interest increased and, although neither the man's person nor his ministry was 'attractive', crowds went out into the wilderness to hear him. It is always significant in any generation when there is a re-emergence of truly biblical ministry. It shows that God is speaking afresh and that he is active. We are reading here the account of a sovereign work of God by his Holy Spirit through the preaching of the Word. There are no man-made revivals. Only God can speak with the voice that wakes the dead and makes people hear. Only God can create soul-thirst and cause people to be concerned about the issues of salvation. The starting point of John's message was repentance and forgiveness. It was not an offer of fulfilment and satisfaction; not a programme to address the wrongs of society, of which there were very many under Roman rule; nor was it a message of 'healing' of various hurts that trouble human life. It was a call to get right with God, to turn away from the sins God was convicting them of, and to come to God with no reliance on human worth or effort, seeking his forgiveness.

John's preaching

Read also John 1:19-37

In Matthew 3:1-10 we are told that John had searching words, addressed particularly to self-righteous religious people who were showing interest, to the effect that if they had genuinely turned to God for salvation then a change in their whole way of life would testify to it. Nowadays many who profess conversion show no real change in their attitudes and activities. Many people responded to John's powerful ministry and made public confession of their dealing with God by being baptized in Jordan. But John was not in any way absorbed with his own success as a preacher, neither at the start of his work nor later on. His concern was to point away from himself to the coming Messiah. Read John 1:19-23,35-37; 3:25-30. Read also Matthew 11:7-11 to see Jesus' testimony to the greatness of John. Now consider the last verse of today's passage. John recognized that repentance and forgiveness do not constitute a full gospel. The forgiven sinner needs to be given the power to withstand and conquer temptation and to bring forth in life the characteristics that prove true conversion. That power is the power of the indwelling Holy Spirit, who is given in his complete and indivisible personality to every believer (Rom. 5:5; Eph. 1:18-20; 3:14-21). We are given new life, new power and new possibility. In the great hymn 'O for a thousand tongues...' Charles Wesley highlights this truth in the words,

> He breaks the power of cancelled sin,
> He sets the prisoner free.

This is the gospel, and John pointed to the only one who can save.

Jesus' baptism

Read also Matthew 3:1-7,11-17

In a situation in which the whole community was being made aware of God and hearing the call of God to repentance and faith, Jesus came amongst the people and was baptized by John. Matthew 3:13-15 records that Jesus said this was part of God's plan. What then is the significance of Jesus' baptism? It is not to be taken as the pattern of our baptism. Nor was it the time (as some suggest) that the man Jesus became the Son of God by the descent and anointing of the Holy Spirit. John's baptism was one of confession of sins and repentance, but Jesus had no sins to repent of. In his thirty years of human life in ordinary circumstances and as a private person, he had been tempted but had not sinned (Heb. 4:15). Now, at the beginning of his public ministry, the Sinless One, by deliberate choice and in a public way, took his place to stand with sinners, making himself one of us and numbering himself with the transgressors (2 Cor. 5:21; Isa. 53:12). He stood in for us sinners, making himself our Representative, so that in due time he could die as our Substitute (1 Peter 3:18; Isa. 53:4-6). There was the need for a Saviour, one to represent sinners and to take their place, and Jesus was the only one who could do this! He came forward and entered the field of battle as our champion. The principle is demonstrated in the story of David, when he took the field as the representative of all the people of Israel against the great enemy Goliath. Think ahead to the time when Jesus stood before Pilate and answered nothing. He accepted the charges on behalf of guilty sinners (John 19:1-11).

The sinless Son

Read also Hebrews 2:14-18; 4:14-16

The emphasis in these verses is on the sinlessness of Jesus. At his baptism, as well as at his death on the cross, he offered himself without spot to God. Spotlessness is not just the absence of sin but the presence of positive moral virtue, tried and proved. In his thirty years in Nazareth Jesus grew from innocence to holiness, and people saw in his person and life all that was true and best in human life, as God had planned in the beginning when man was first made in the image of God. To be truly human, and to be God's 'proper man' (Luther) for the work of redemption, Jesus had to be tempted in all points just as we are. And he was tempted comprehensively, knowing the power of temptation to an infinitely greater degree than we have ever known; we yield and fall long before temptation has reached its full power. In all these years, as a true man made in the likeness of sinful flesh (Rom. 8:3, AV), there was never the slightest deflection from God in thought, motive or desire. As a man, he took his stand with sinners in order to win the victory for us. It was in this context that God spoke and declared his pleasure in his eternal Son. Who can imagine the pleasure of the Father in his Son as he watched him down the years of childhood, in adolescence and then manhood? Who can imagine the Father's pleasure as he heard the words, 'I must be about my Father's business' (Luke 2:49, AV)? Who can imagine the Father's heart as, in the very shadow of the cross, Jesus spoke the words in John 17:4? What must it have been like to live in Nazareth alongside Jesus? It is said that we grow to be like the people we keep company with. In studying the Gospel narrative we keep company with Jesus.

The Saviour tempted

Read also Luke 4:1-13

What Mark records with startling brevity is told in great detail in Matthew 4:1-11 and Luke 4:1-13, where the full range and nature of the temptations are dealt with. Matthew and Luke tell how Satan tempted Jesus to turn from the way of the obedience of faith. The temptation was to use signs, miracles and 'stunts' to win people's response. Jesus' reliance on the truth of Scripture won his total victory, causing the tempter to depart until his next opportunity (Luke 4:13). Mark's emphasis is different. He wants us to see that the initiative was totally with God. It was the Spirit who drove Jesus into the wilderness. Jesus was acutely aware that confronting the devil was a necessary consequence of taking his place as representative man. In John Henry Newman's words, in the hymn 'Praise to the holiest', this was the 'second Adam' come to the fight and rescue. It is better to think of Jesus as the last Adam (1 Cor. 15:45), come to rectify the disaster created by the fall of the first Adam. Jesus went into the wilderness, away from people, into the lonely, barren wastes that seem to symbolize the devil's territory. The first Adam was in God's garden with the animals tame and under his lordship. Jesus was in a desert, with none of the comforts of Eden, but with the atmosphere of sinful fallenness, and with the beasts wild and dangerous. It was into the real world of fallen humanity, fallen nature and satanic dominion, that Jesus came to turn the whole kingdom of evil upside down. And it was as a man, not a superhuman divine being, that he did so. The reference to forty days indicates something of the length and intensity of the temptation and, according to Matthew 4:11, it was after the battle was fought and won in glorious isolation that the angels ministered to Jesus.

The enemy defeated

Read also Matthew 4:12-17

There is a dramatic intensity in the narrative. John baptized Jesus. The Champion took centre stage. The enemy was challenged in a confrontation he may well have wanted to avoid at that stage. Having been faced and conquered in the one-to-one battle in the wilderness, the devil then, by manipulation of wicked men and women, caused the mighty voice of John the Baptist to be silenced. While we do not minimize the terrible things the devil does accomplish, this was not a decisive victory for Satan. He is a real enemy, and always angry (Rev. 12:12), but at the very time that John's voice was silenced, Jesus' voice takes up the same message. Mark emphasizes that this ministry now begun is in full accord with what has gone before. There is no conflict between Old and New Testaments. What was now happening was the fulfilment of what had been promised and prepared for through the generations of the Old Testament and it was all coming to pass at God's instigation. Jesus was not waiting for things to happen, he was causing them to happen, having set all the events in motion when he stepped forward to be baptized by John. This emphasis on God's initiative runs right through Mark's Gospel. When we are told that the kingdom of God is near, we are not to think of a territorial area ruled by a king, but rather of the activity of a king who has come among men. Mark is saying that the King is here. Jesus is speaking the good news of God and calling people to repent and believe. This King Jesus is the one who is able to forgive sins, to break the power of evil, and to set sinners free. Of course, the presence of Jesus always calls for response, and it is as we believe in him that we find the power to turn from our sinful ways. We become subjects of the Saviour King.

The first disciples

Read also John 1:35-51

The King begins to recruit his executive workers, and the scene has moved from Judea and Jerusalem to the northern area of Galilee. In spite of the success of the Baptist's ministry, there was no move by Jesus to force a confrontation with the religious or secular governments of Jerusalem. His ministry was 'time-tabled' and this is something to remember for our comfort and reassurance when we are perplexed (v. 15; Gal. 4:4; John 7:6,8,30; Eccles. 3:1-8). The disciples were neither volunteers nor conscripts. They were called personally and, as Mark records, responded immediately without prior preparation. This should not surprise us, because the work of the Holy Spirit is sovereign and effective. At the same time, in John 1:35-44, we find an account of how some of the Baptist's disciples, Andrew, Peter and, we think, the unnamed John, were in contact with Jesus and having conversations with him. This is very encouraging for all who preach or teach. These men were first influenced by John the Baptist, who made plain that his work was to prepare his listeners for ministry that was yet to come. In due time, the 'seed' of John's earlier words was kindled into powerful life in the seemingly accidental incident as Jesus passed along by the Sea of Galilee and saw the two men at work. In our contact with people we have no idea what other influences have been at work in their lives. Our words and actions can become links in the chain of God's grace at work to bring forth spiritual fruit. We are always entering into other people's spiritual labours (John 4:38) and passing on the work to others. There are no casual visitors to our churches nor casual meetings in the course of the day. We need to be ready to be used by God.

Called to serve

Read also Luke 5:1-11

If John had had previous contact with Jesus, perhaps his brother James and their father had also heard from and been influenced by him. Zebedee certainly did not seem surprised, and raised no objection when his two sons responded to the call of Jesus. It must have meant disruption to and reorganization of the family fishing business. It may also have meant a commitment to his sons on Zebedee's part, to back them and support them in their full-time service. Note that there is an indication here that not all Jesus' disciples were poor people. This family owned a boat, and we read in Luke 8:1-4 that some found their spiritual service in providing the means for others to serve. Compared with the crowds that followed John, Jesus seems to have had a very low-key start in his ministry, which is in full swing in the next verses. But it is all very exciting. Jesus did not call important people, that is, important in worldly terms, but he did call people with capacities that could be developed for the particular service they were called to. This does not mean that only those with special gifts are called to Jesus for salvation. That would be a total denial of the gospel. But it does mean that Jesus calls people to the kind of service for which their natural gifts and capacities can be developed and trained by the enabling power of the Holy Spirit, as they are taught by God through his Word. Jesus made his intentions quite clear when he said to these fishermen that he would make them become fishers of men. Note that he did not say to them, 'Use your gifts, natural and spiritual, express them in my service and you will be useful to God.' Even on the human level they had to learn their limitations and inabilities (Luke 5:1-11). Their usefulness lay in their following Jesus.

Personalities and potential

Read also 2 Corinthians 4:7-12; 12:1-10

Read these five verses again. Peter, James and John, whose natural personalities were turbulent, could have ended up a danger to the work, apart from Jesus. Even in companionship with Jesus and under his personal instruction, Peter did the devil's work (Mark 8:31-33) and James and John were wild and ambitious (Luke 9:49-55; Mark 10:35-41). Andrew was the quiet man, usually overshadowed by his more gifted brother, but on a personal level he did great service. He brought people to Jesus: Peter in John 1:41, the boy with the loaves and fishes (John 6:8), and the Greeks (John 12:20). As we follow Jesus, hearing his Word, learning from his dealings with us, we become men and women trained and prepared for the service that is planned for us. Unpredictable Peter became a rocklike character (John 1:42). Fiery John became the apostle of love and the saintly seer of the Book of Revelation (John 13:25; 1 John 3:1-2; Rev. 1:9). Jesus can take the most unpromising people, those devalued by their contemporaries and regarded as having no potential, and make them a means of blessing to others. Of course, such training and development is never without its cost. When Jesus said he would make these disciples fishers of men they knew that becoming good fishermen depended not just on inbred capacity but on hard work, patience, preparation, knowledge, discipline and an ability to cope with disappointment. Fishermen can lose their nets, and even their boat, and that can mean starting all over again. But none of the disappointments, or even the disasters, need frustrate the purpose of Jesus, so long as we keep following. The costly experiences are often the secret source of our usefulness (2 Cor. 4:7-12; 12:1-10).

The true preacher

Read also Luke 4:14-22

Beginning at verse 21 we have the record of the events on a crowded Sabbath day and Mark emphasizes the urgency and immediacy of every phase. Jesus had been a regular attender at the synagogue in Nazareth and was known as one who could teach (Luke 4:14-22). He would have waited to be called on by the leader of the synagogue in Capernaum. We should not think of Jesus simply barging in and taking over. That is an attitude scarcely calculated to make a congregation receptive, and ministers and others need to remember this. No doubt Jesus taught from the passage of Scripture appointed for that day and what impressed everyone was the authority his words carried. This was not the impact of eloquence, personality or argument, but the unction of heaven by the Holy Spirit. There was undoubtedly grace as well as truth (John 1:14). But there was power. You cannot imagine Jesus trying to impress or to create an 'atmosphere', by manipulation of voice, tone or gesticulation. That would be more psychological manipulation than preaching God's Word. Jesus spoke in the synagogue as the servant of God and of his Word, and, because there was no desire, conscious or unconscious, to minister to 'self', there was no hindrance to the Word going forth freely to do its work. Whether in pulpits, Sunday school classes, youth clubs or wherever, we need to have confidence in God's Word and allow it to stand in its own right and power. We need to remember that God's Word carries its own authority and does its own work (Isa. 55:10-11; 1 Thess. 2:13). It does not need 'worldly' or carnal additions or adornments to make it acceptable (2 Cor. 10:3-4). Of course, those who handle God's Word must be right and clean in themselves (Isa. 52:11).

An outburst of evil

Read also Ephesians 6:10-20

Not all in the congregation were impressed in the same
way with the words and authority of Jesus. The preaching
produced an outburst of reaction from one particular man,
who may have been a regular attender and who, prior to
this incident, may never have shown any sign of anything
unusual. He may not have known that he was in the grip of
evil, and both the people and rulers of the synagogue may
have been taken aback by his fierce outburst. We are dealing here with the objective reality of evil and the invasion
of human lives by its spirits, but we must not assume that
the powers of evil had just at that moment taken hold on
the man. Nor must we assume that evil always manifests
itself in wild and frightening ways. Think of the cold, calculating attitude of the Pharisees and the relentless build-up
of their determination to kill Jesus. Think also of the cul-
tured, insensitive spirit of Judas that persisted and grew,
even in the inner circle of Jesus' disciples. Evil can be religious, refined, intellectual and even moral. But when it is
confronted by the power of the word of the gospel it reacts.
Think of the reaction of many against any attempt to affirm
biblical standards of life and behaviour. Think of the outbursts of mockery against any who try to restrict human
indulgence. Think of the fiendish words spoken against
what people tend to call 'Puritanism'. Then consider here
how the evil spirit convulsed the man before yielding its
grip on him. Evil does not give up easily, even in the presence of Jesus. But note also the authority of Jesus: the
recognition by the evil spirits that Jesus had the power to
destroy them, and the fact that Jesus commanded. He did
not discuss or argue. There was nothing theatrical about
his actions.

Jesus in an ordinary home

Read also Luke 10:38-42

The scene moves from the synagogue to Peter's house and we see Jesus, who taught with authority and who confronted the powers of evil and cast them out, now in an ordinary domestic situation. It may have been only on arriving home that Peter discovered that his mother-in-law was struck down with fever. They did the natural thing. They told Jesus, and discovered immediately that he cared. The woman was healed. The action of taking her by the hand, with no words or signs of power, must have touched the hearts of all present. Mark's comment that she then waited on them, no doubt helping to prepare a meal as the rest sat and talked, tells of a supremely natural family gathering in which Jesus was quite at ease. He fitted in. He is happy to sit at table with those who want his company. We could use this story as a parable showing Jesus as the one who draws away the fever of life, brings peace, and restores life and service to us. Perhaps Peter's mother-in-law knew that Jesus and his disciples were coming and you can imagine her fretting and being distressed because she was unwell and not able to entertain. But the presence of Jesus brought enabling. There is no need to fret, no need for tension, when he is in the home. His presence brings peace. Is it too mundane to think that instead of healing the woman Jesus might well have gone to the kitchen and helped to prepare the meal? If our spirituality keeps us from doing that kind of task there is something wrong. How we should give thanks for a truly human Jesus! He fits in so well, wherever he is wanted.

When the sun had set

Read also Matthew 4:23-28

At sundown, the Sabbath was officially over and the people felt free to come to see this Jesus who had cast out the demon from the man in the synagogue, and they brought the sick, needy and demon-possessed to him. We are not told how they decided that someone had a demon. Perhaps they were as arbitrary as some people in our own day, diagnosing almost any disorder in terms of demonology. We do not deny the reality of evil spirits, nor the fact that the presence of Jesus draws hidden evil out into the open. But we must note that Jesus forbade the spirits to speak even though they recognized who he was (v. 24). It may be that Jesus silenced the demons in order to prevent them from putting themselves centre stage and focusing attention on themselves rather than on Jesus. In some areas of evangelical activity today there is a preoccupation with demonology and exorcism, which leads to a neglect of all other aspects of the person, power and teaching of the Lord Jesus Christ. If we ponder today's verses and keep in mind the hurt and longings of human nature, we realize that many would have come to seek Jesus only in order to find relief and escape from things that tormented and tyrannized their lives. Jesus can give relief, and does so for many, but this does not necessarily mean that people come to saving faith. But when we do come to Jesus in saving faith then there is no limit to the healing, delivering and fulfilling work he can do in our personalities and lives. He can change us almost beyond recognition. And with what gentleness and understanding he heals our hurt and brokenness!

Sleep and prayer

Read also Matthew 14:22-23; Philippians 4:4-7

We are not told when the crowd finally departed but, because he was human, Jesus would recognize the need for sleep. Jesus also recognized the need for prayer and quiet communion with God his Father. For that reason, very early in the morning, without waking everyone else, he left the house to spend time in undisturbed prayer. We are not told what he prayed about. Did he commit to God both the work done the previous day, and the day's activities about to begin? The emphasis is certainly on praying rather than on the very early morning. Some pray best at night. Some pray when they should be asleep and some sleep when they should be praying. The need is for balance and discipline, because without these we can feel too busy to pray or run ourselves into a state of exhaustion in which we are easy targets for the devil. He is an expert at using genuine zeal for the Lord to make us less and less able and fit to serve him. Here we learn from Jesus that a right relationship with God is the heart of all our service. In due time, possibly because Jesus was absent from breakfast, the others went to look for him. When they found him their excitement was great, but there was almost a note of rebuke in their words because there was already a crowd, no doubt drawn by the previous night's miracles and looking for more demonstrations of power. Already the disciples were showing signs of being captivated by success. Already there are signs that Simon Peter was becoming the quick spokesman. The disciples must have been taken aback by Jesus' decision to go on to the next towns, but note that he said, 'Let us go'. They were his chosen men and part of his planned work. Their limited understanding did not exclude them from further developments.

Priorities

Read also Romans 10:8-15

The pattern of Jesus' ministry teaches important lessons. The disciples were overexcited by the success of the miracles and the subsequent crowds, and Jesus took them away. He knew how people can become fascinated by miracles and want more of them. But we must remember that not all miracles are worked by the good power of God, nor do they prove that God is at work, nor do they necessarily lead to faith (Matt. 11:20-24; 7:21-23; cf. Exod. 4:8-12). The disciples were shown that neither the desires of the people nor their own desires were to be allowed to direct or control the work of the gospel. They were taught also that in the ongoing work of God preaching, not miracle working, must be central. Yes, along with the preaching there was the manifestation of God's power to heal and deliver human lives. But it was the proclamation of God's Word that was to take priority. This is something that all preachers must be clear about. There are so many things that can claim time and energy that often both mind and spirit are tired before preachers settle down to study and to prepare for ministering God's Word in a way that will bring the very bread of life to hungry people. Shallow preaching becomes dull and tasteless and, alas, for too many, preaching has become the Cinderella activity. The disciples were not yet aware that the work of God is long term, and they were tempted to snatch at immediate local success. Perhaps this is one reason for Jesus' early morning praying. There could have been a repeat of the temptations in the wilderness, offering popular success. But converts won by commotion seldom last! Be clear about this. Prayer is the heart of true ministry, but a minister cannot do all the preaching and all the praying alone.

Drawn by the preaching

Read also 2 Kings 5:1-5,10-14; John 4:46-54

The leper seems to have come to Jesus as a result of the preaching recorded in the previous passage. Nowadays the effectiveness of preaching in bringing people into contact with Jesus tends to be ignored, and as a result all sorts of 'methods' are resorted to in order to attract people. But God is active in his Word and it is the work of the Holy Spirit to draw people under the sound of that Word. The leper, whose disease would have been obvious and would have made him a social and religious outcast, seemed to have had no doubt as to Jesus' capacity to heal, but he doubted his willingness. Perhaps he felt that a man like Jesus would see no value in someone like him. He felt rejected by society because he *was* rejected, and perhaps this had caused him to feel worthless in himself. Even the hope that some change might happen was something of a miracle. It is a very human story, and in it we see the wonderful compassion of Jesus. No one would touch a leper, but Jesus did, and that was the first step in restoring the man's dignity and sense of worth. The leper's hesitation did not deter Jesus. He did not wait for perfect faith or understanding. Jesus answered the man's plea saying, 'I can, and I will.' The leper was healed immediately. The power of Jesus was unquestionable. What is impossible in the eyes of men is possible with God.

Unwise publicity

Read also Leviticus 14:1-32

Jesus' stern injunction not to make a public fuss calls into question the modern tendency to publicize everything that might possibly suggest that the church is a success. Jesus' counsel was wise psychologically, because the man would be very excited and that can be a dangerous condition. It was spiritually wise, in that he was sent to the priest (whether locally or in Jerusalem) to offer the appropriate sacrifice required by the law of Moses (Lev. 14:1-32). This would signify that Jesus' ministry was not something new, but emerging out of the Old Testament preparation. As far as he could, Jesus gave the religious establishment of his day its proper place, so long as it was true to God and his Word. The counsel to be silent was also wise practically. It would soon be seen that the cure had happened. But what the man had to do was to show, not just by his changed condition, but by his ongoing changed life, that he had been to Jesus and that he had found salvation and life in him. What actually happened was that the man's foolish enthusiasm, which may have been short-lived (high emotion seldom lasts) created such an excited commotion that the ongoing work of Jesus was hindered. Enthusiasm has to be controlled or else, as in this case, it may become an instrument of Satan.

Determined friends

Read also Genesis 18:20-33

After some time spent in other areas, where he still could not escape the crowds (1:45), Jesus returned to Capernaum. The house was congested inside and outside, and Jesus was teaching. We are not told his theme: an exposition of an Old Testament passage, or perhaps something like the Sermon on the Mount. Then there came the astonishing interruption when the man on the mat was lowered down into the immediate presence of Jesus. We do not know if the man had asked his friends to take him to Jesus or if he had protested all the way as they carried him. The determination the friends showed and the effort they expended were marvellous. Nothing was going to prevent them bringing this needy man to Jesus. This does not mean that it is right to force people to come to church but there is a lesson here on prayer. We can bring people in need right into Jesus' presence by prayer. We are not told whether the friends actually said anything, just that they simply lowered the man down and looked to Jesus. Jesus saw their faith. Did he look up at the four men who were looking down through the roof, and then look at the man lying at his feet? Whose faith is referred to? Was it the faith of all five, that is, corporate faith? Was it vicarious faith, the faith of friends standing in for the man who was not yet able or willing to believe for himself? No one can stand in for another in terms of saving faith, but we read in Genesis 19:29 that God remembered Abraham (who prayed) and delivered Lot. Think of a prayer meeting where individual faith can be strengthened and weak faith upheld. Keep in mind that as we pray we are not alone; Jesus Christ is our constant intercessor (Rom. 8:34; Heb. 7:25).

An unexpected answer

Read also Matthew 9:1-8

The occasion was public but very personal. The paralytic looked to Jesus. His faith may have been feeble, uncertain and untaught, but it was faith. Jesus also saw that his need was deeper than just the healing of his body and he spoke with great and gentle kindness (Matt. 9:2), saying, 'Your sins are forgiven', fully, finally, as of now. The man, the friends and the crowd may all have been shocked by such direct speaking. Many, including the five men, may have felt this was a poor outcome compared to physical healing, and their faces may have shown disappointment. They may even have wondered if some guilty secret lay at the root of the man's paralysis. The man perhaps thought his friends had divulged his secret, told to them in confidence (a most cruel thing to do, except when speaking to God alone in prayer). There is no doubt that guilt can paralyse a human life, body as well as personality. Perhaps only Jesus and the man knew what was being spoken of, and the man must have felt instant relief and release when Jesus spoke, not words of condemnation, nor advice, but free and total forgiveness. Forgiveness is a blessing to the whole of life, even if bodily healing does not accompany it. We must be very careful not to attribute all sickness and personality disorder to specific, personal sin. Job's friends did that and they were totally wrong (Job 1:1,8; 2:3). Jesus taught this lesson in John 9:1-3. We live with fallen human nature in a fallen world and there will always be mysteries that we simply cannot explain. In this man's experience Jesus brought forgiveness and broke the power of cancelled sin, so that he got up and walked. The friends went home together knowing all the effort had been well worthwhile.

29

The prejudice of unbelief

Read also Hebrews 3:7-18

There is a dark side to this story. Not all were thrilled by Jesus' teaching and his word of forgiveness. The scribes were 'sitting there', scowling and critical, accusing Jesus of blasphemy because, as they said rightly, only God has the authority to forgive. Their unbelief was total. They simply did not believe that Jesus was God the eternal Son, sent into the world by the Father to be the Saviour of sinners. Everything hinges on what we believe about Jesus. If he is simply a teacher, one of the prophets, or an example of loving morality, then he has no right to speak as if he has divine authority. In spite of their orthodox religion these teachers were simply unable to recognize that God had come amongst them. They had already experienced the power and authority of Jesus' ministry (1:23-27). Perhaps the healed leper had testified to them in the synagogue (1:44). These men did not enquire of Jesus so that their uncertainties might be enlightened. They sat and criticized him inwardly. He was not part of their religious system, although he had been invited to speak in the synagogue (1:21-22). They did not recognize his credentials even though they knew *they* did not have God's unction on their preaching as he had (Matt. 7:28-29). This is the prejudice of unbelief. Jesus challenged them with the question in verse 9, and before they could answer he spoke to the man the word of command and the paralytic rose and walked. The visible miracle confirmed the hidden work of forgiveness and made plain that Jesus was what he claimed to be, the Son of God, the Saviour of the world. We are told that the crowd was amazed and glorified God. But did the religious teachers believe? Their unbelief appears with increasing intensity right through the story. Beware unbelief! (Heb. 3:12-13).

The tax man converted

Read also Matthew 21:28-32

Levi is Matthew (Matt. 9:9), a man well trained in writing
and keeping accurate accounts, and therefore well prepared
to write a full account of the life and ministry of Jesus.
These two verses tell the beginning of his life of discipleship. There had been general astonishment in Capernaum
regarding the words and works of Jesus and, no doubt, Levi
would have heard all about it as the people came to pay
their taxes. Mark emphasizes the ongoing nature of Jesus'
ministry in the word 'again' and adds that he was preaching beside the sea. There was a tax-office as a lot of money
was taken in by levies on trade. It almost seems accidental
that Jesus saw Levi but God's dealings are never casual.
Jesus spoke and, to everyone's astonishment, Levi got up,
left his job, and followed him. Now Levi was a renegade
Jew employed by the Roman government and would be regarded by the people, and certainly by the religious leaders, as a traitor to the Jewish nation and therefore a traitor
to the faith of the fathers. But, while the orthodox refused
Jesus, this man responded. The Holy Spirit may well have
been troubling Levi for a long time, awakening in mind
and heart things he had been taught in his younger days,
and creating in him a spirit of longing for a different life.
We are often unaware of much of God's activity and should
not judge people as *we* see them. As the work of the gospel
goes on, we may be expecting the wrong kind of people to
respond. Consider Jesus' words in Matthew 21:28-32! What
did Peter, Andrew, James and John, well-taught disciples of
John the Baptist before following Jesus, think when Jesus
called Levi to join them? How do we react when 'outsiders'
come to church and prove to be more eager and committed
than those who have been coming a long time?

31

The dinner party

Read also Luke 15:1-7

We are told in Luke 5:29-32 that soon after he had answered the call of Jesus, Levi made a feast in his own house and invited a considerable company of people, including many of the tax-collectors, and many referred to as 'sinners', not necessarily grossly immoral people but those who had abandoned the rigorous, legal religion of the Pharisees. There may have been an 'open' invitation. I recall once being in Jerusalem with my family, watching from a distance an open-air wedding reception, and being told that we should join in and no one would object. In Levi's house and garden there was an interesting company of 'sinners' and we cannot but wonder why the Pharisees were there. Was it because they made it their business to keep in with the people who had a lot of money? Jesus once made a biting comment about the commercialism of their religion and accused them of hypocrisy (Mark 12:38-40). Perhaps the Pharisees felt it was their spiritual duty to spy on people who might be doing wrong! At Levi's feast, what the Pharisees failed to see, let alone to understand, was a company of people who were aware of their need: not just a hunger for life that satisfied, but a deep-seated awareness of the need to be right with God. It is when people know that they are 'sick' that they look for the kind of Physician who can heal them in the depth of their souls. We need to be careful that in the work of the gospel we do not deal just with the individual and social consequences of sin. We must get to the heart of the need, which is to be right with God. Read Luke 15:1-2. Some people have no sense of need.

Fasting

Read also Luke 18:9-14

John's disciples and the Pharisees had this in common, that they both regarded fasting as important. But the Pharisees boasted about their fasting (Luke 18:9-14), a contradiction of the essential element in fasting, which is denial of self, not just missing a few meals. John's disciples were stern with themselves, denying all that could be regarded as creature comforts. They copied the lifestyle of their teacher, perhaps failing to see that personalities differ and that what to one man is authentic self-denial towards God, can to another be an expression of self. Granted, as John made plain, repentance and faith should manifest themselves in a lifestyle that is no longer self-centred and indulgent but seeks to please and honour God. However, when both groups of fasting men considered Jesus and his disciples, they were disturbed by the fact that these men seemed to enjoy the life of faith and discipleship. They were perplexed by this, confusing a gloomy attitude with spirituality. They felt that a true relationship with God was in essence a case of being sorry for sins, and they were offering their fasting to God as a way of 'making up' for their sins. But the forgiveness Jesus brings puts away sins, gets them out of the way, consigning them to oblivion so that they no longer cast a shadow between us and God (Micah 7:19; 1 John 1:7-9). How can God possibly enjoy fellowship with those he has ransomed and redeemed, if they are always talking about their sins, preoccupied with them rather than with the Saviour? This is not to make light of sin and failure. We dare not be careless. There must be a turning away from sin and a dying to sin (Rom. 6:1-14). But sin must not become the dominant focus of our lives. Jesus is the focus.

Fulness of life

Read also John 10:1-10

The presence of Jesus in the lives of forgiven sinners is likened to the happiness of a wedding. It is to be enjoyed. Think of the joy, peace, hope, deliverance and transformation he has brought into our lives! We should count our blessings and recognize that all we now have and enjoy is ours in him and in him alone. Times do come when, in the interest of spiritual service, there has to be radical self-denial in areas of natural and legitimate fulfilment (1 Cor. 7:1-5). At times we must set a stern guard in those areas of temptation where we know we are vulnerable (1 Peter 2:11). There are times when we must suffer greatly for the sake of Jesus and the gospel (2 Cor. 4:7-12; Phil. 3:7-11). But when that is our lot, we must, as far as we are able, put a good face on it, lest we simply attract attention to ourselves (Matt. 6:1-4,16-18). At such times, if we are wise and honest, we will share the burden with some who are close to us and trustworthy. But Jesus has come so that we may have life in full measure in this world and the next (John 10:10). His objective is to transform our lives totally and so to develop our personalities that we are able to receive all that he longs to give, full measure, pressed down and running over! Jesus is not a patch to be added to improve life here and there and make it more bearable. Jesus makes all things new. He cannot be fitted into old patterns and containers. This does not mean we throw away all the well-proven patterns of worship and service because that, too often, is simply to institute novelty. Secular words can express this spiritual truth: 'Wider still and wider shall thy bounds be set.' The old hymn has it, 'More and more, more and more, still there's more to follow.' There is no limit to what Jesus can do, and wants to do, with the life he has given us.

God's Sabbath

Read also 1 Samuel 21:1-6

The central message of this passage is not the institution of
the Sabbath, nor the right way to observe it, but the persistent enmity of the Pharisees. Here they are seen following
Jesus and the disciples with the specific intention of spying on them in order to find some way of accusing him,
and them, of opposing God and his laws. The obsessive
legalism of the religion of the Pharisees is revealed as they
regarded the plucking of a few heads of grain as 'working'
and even 'harvesting' on the Sabbath. The same arbitrary
attitudes prevail today when some things done in the home
are regarded as permissible but as wrong if done outside
where people might see. The Pharisees were spying and
had hate in their hearts, but they did not consider *that*
wrong! According to them they were doing it for God, to
guard his Sabbath. When they challenged Jesus about his
disciples' actions, he answered them with a factual account
from 1 Samuel 21:1-6 about King David whom the Pharisees revered. David, servant of God, persecuted by his
enemies, was given the holy bread by the priest, who considered the circumstances warranted such an action. There
was need, and therefore mercy allowed the relaxing of the
strict letter of the law. Here there was also need for food as
the disciples followed Jesus. Works of mercy and necessity
are allowed on the Sabbath, and that is made plain if we
read Matthew 12:11-12 in the context of the next story Mark
tells (3:1-6). Jesus' words here in verse 27 have been taken
by many to argue against the 'Keep Sunday Special' cam-
paign, but verse 28 corrects the balance. Jesus is Lord of
the Sabbath, and it is in glad submission to his Lordship
that we find the blessing of the Sabbath.

Sabbath blessing

Read also Isaiah 58:13-14; Jeremiah 17:19-27

In considering this incident it is useful to read the further passages suggested for today. Our attitude to the Sabbath must be neither legalistic nor dismissive, because it was made for man, as a blessing and a safeguard, not a burden and denial. God's law says we must remember to keep the Sabbath, not just to observe it, but to fulfil its God-given function. This special day began in the order of creation, long before the Ten Commandments, and it is built into God's order of things. In the final act of creation God made man; then he blessed the seventh day and ordained it for the enjoyment, benefit and satisfaction of the fellowship he planned and desired to have with man. God rested, and in like manner we who believe rest in the finished work of Christ, and are able to rejoice in it with unfailing regularity on God's Sabbath, the Lord's Day. Those who drive themselves on seven days in the week, ignoring God's institution, distort the whole order of life as God meant it to be. Without a true Sabbath, life and society disintegrate, and we must view with concern the pressures of secular interests to destroy Sunday. We need God's ordained day in order to stop, to focus our minds and hearts on him, and to remember that man does not live by bread alone. If we give ourselves to the business of this world we may well be in the process of losing our souls (Luke 12:13-21). This means we need to prepare for God's Sabbath, ordering our whole week so as to gain the blessing for which his day was made. We are more important than the day, but we must never misuse or distort it. As we learn to love the Lord and walk with him, we will know how to use this holy day to honour him, not least by the witness of our lives to the effect that what pleases God comes first.

Healing on the Sabbath

Read also Matthew 23:1-15

This passage completes the story of a succession of six conflicts between the Pharisees and Jesus (2:6,16,18,24; 3:2,6). In spite of having seen and heard all Jesus' wonderful words and works, these men were further away from God than ever. Despite that, and knowing the formalism and hypocrisy of the religion of the synagogue, Jesus still went there to worship. This does not mean we should always stay in a congregation where the person and word of Jesus are dishonoured. We should find an alternative if possible, even if it is socially less convenient. In Capernaum the synagogue was the only gathering place for worship and if Jesus had not attended, his action would have been misunderstood. As soon as he entered the building he saw the man with the shrivelled hand, who may even have been 'planted' there by Jesus' enemies to show that in God's house he disregarded God and his Law. There was no spirit of worship among many who 'watched' to see what Jesus would do, nor any real interest in the poor man's misery. They would not have lifted a hand to help him because it was the Sabbath. Jesus accepted the obvious challenge not just to heal the man but to expose the hypocrisy of the leaders. How did the man himself feel? We can imagine his trembling response when Jesus called him to stand up, and his thrill and delight when life came back to his dead hand. Without doubt, the reactions in the congregation were divided. Between faith and unbelief there is a great, and eternal, gulf. Some rejoiced, but the Pharisees determined all the more to destroy Jesus. Note Jesus' anger at those who are a barrier to people coming to faith (Matt. 23:1-15), and his grief at the hard unbelief of so many hearts. We should think more often of the Jesus who weeps (Luke 9:41; Matt. 23:37).

Practical spirituality

Read also Luke 14:28-35

Jesus withdrew along with his disciples to avoid unnecessary confrontation, and to teach his disciples that short-term success must not replace God's long-term purposes. Jesus did not in fact escape from the crowds, who were drawn by all he was doing. The commotion surrounding Jesus could be likened to the excitement and pressure of crowds crushing to see, hear and even touch their 'pop idols'. Maintaining his composure Jesus assessed the situation and asked the disciples to have a boat ready so that, if necessary, he could board it and be able to be seen and heard by all. There are lessons here that show that the life of faith is not simply trusting God that all will work out. Jesus thought ahead and considered the situation in a practical way. We must do the same. If we feel God is calling us to some particular sphere of service in the gospel we must not rush into it. We must think of the practicalities. If we feel a call to the ministry, are we already learning how to study and handle Scripture? If we feel a call to the mission field, have we considered health, capacity to learn a language, and under what auspices we may enter another country? Spiritual enthusiasm is good, but it must be married to clear thinking. We have seen Jesus silence the evil spirits in the notes on 1:23-28 and 32-34. Here we simply emphasize the total mastery of Jesus over evil, in its wild outbursts and cold calculating resistance to his person and his word. What the evil spirits said was true. But Jesus would have no part with those, demonic or human, whose motivation and objectives were totally contrary to his God-given commission. We need to be careful before we get involved with people who seem spiritual but who may have no part in Christ and the gospel (Matt. 7:21-23; 1 John 4:1).

Called to be with Jesus

Read also John 15:1-6

According to Luke 6:12-16, it was after a night of prayer that Jesus chose these twelve men out of a larger company. He called to himself those he wanted. It is great to feel needed but even greater to feel wanted. Jesus called these men to be with him, and it was from being with him, in loving and learning fellowship, that they were sent out to be significant workers for God in the world. It is our personal relationship with the Lord Jesus, the quality of our walk with him, that determines the quality, extent and fruitfulness of our service. Read John 15:1-6 and ponder the sad end of Judas Iscariot, who sold Jesus to his enemies. Think of other disciples, for in Jesus' experience, as in Paul's, many went back from their earlier commitment to service (John 6:66-71; 2 Tim. 4:9-16). It is sad when people depart from the *edge* of the work of the gospel but it is sore indeed when they depart from the *heart* of the work, and, saddest of all, when one at the heart of the work is revealed to have been a servant of Satan right from the start. It is little wonder that in the upper room the disciples said, 'Lord, is it I?' These men were chosen and called and therefore valued, and this must have been an ongoing assurance to them when they were assailed by feelings of failure, inferiority and limitation. Jesus wants us for ourselves, not just to make use of us in his service. These men were sent out with a given authority that extended to cover the area of demonic activity. Delegated authority is never our own to use as and when we feel inclined. Nor does it signify spiritual superiority. In our persons and our service we have only what has been given to us in trust (1 Cor. 4:7). The disciples were sent to preach, and their authority over demons was in the authority of the Word preached, rather than in forms of exorcism.

The chosen ones

Read also Matthew 16:13-16,21-28

Consider the various characters and stories of some of the disciples. Peter talked too much at times, was too sure of his own spirituality, and had a capacity for blundering as well as for discernment and leadership (Matt. 16:13-16, 21-28). James and John had thundery temperaments, yet John became the apostle of love. Andrew was a great one-to-one worker (John 1:40-42; 6:8-9). Philip was slow to grasp things (John 14:8). Thomas always saw the black side of things (John 11:16). Simon was a nationalist and possibly his politics coloured his spiritual attitudes: something we need to be careful about, just as we need to watch that personal friendships do not unbalance our spiritual assessments. Jesus' choice of Judas remains a mystery. No one seemed to have had doubts about him, but Jesus knew what was hidden from others. Two things are clear. Evil, in the person of Judas, right at the heart of the work, never disturbed or distracted Jesus and, at the critical development of the work as the time for the cross drew near, Jesus showed his complete mastery over evil. We have no way of knowing what Judas' feelings were when Jesus said, 'What you are about to do, do quickly' (John 13:27). Judas did not hesitate, but went straight to the high priest with whom he had made his evil bargain (Matt. 26:14-16). Was Judas a man sold out to the devil right from the start, an object of wrath fitted for destruction (Rom. 9:22), an example of intrinsic evil brought within the working of God in order to serve the purpose of his mercy and salvation? We must not go beyond what the Bible teaches clearly. Certainly Judas was chosen to be with Jesus, and yet every step of the way he moved further and further away. Beware the hardening of heart that leads to cynical unbelief (Heb. 3:12-13).

Misunderstood by family

Read also Luke 2:39-52

Jesus and the disciples had gone to the quiet seclusion of the hills where the Twelve were chosen and commissioned. They then returned home to Capernaum and before very long there was again a crowd, so pressing that there was no time to eat. This could be regarded as continuing success but in fact it was a dangerous situation, because it put both Jesus and his disciples under unreasonable pressure that could have endangered the long-term continuance of the work. If the choosing of the Twelve had been a significant new development of Jesus' ministry, we have to discern the immediate reaction of Satan, seeking to hinder and disturb. This is confirmed by the radical reaction of Jesus' friends, who seem to have been his 'family'. They may have had the best of intentions, being persuaded that he would harm himself if he went on as he was doing. They went out to take charge of him because they thought he was out of his mind. These 'friends' wanted to restrict or even stop Jesus' activity, which shows that they must have totally failed to recognize the spiritual validity and significance of the man whom they had known for so many years. We know nothing of Jesus' life at home prior to his public ministry, except from Luke 2:40-52. Was he so very 'ordinary' that they never suspected he was anything special? Were they jealous that he had become such a public figure? Were they out of sympathy with all he said and did (John 7:5)? If the family had heard his teaching and seen his miracles, why did they not react as so many others did (Matt. 7:28-29; 12:23)? Think of the loneliness and the hurt Jesus felt within his own family circle. If you are the only believer in your family, Jesus understands!

In league with the devil

Read also John 7:40-52

First the crowd, then the family, and now the teachers of the Law are seen as instruments of Satan. The crowds were carried away by their own enthusiasm. The family was moved by exasperation and perhaps resentment. Now the religious enemies, motivated by bitterness and hate, quite deliberately put an evil interpretation on the person and the work of Jesus. They had seen Jesus' power to heal; authority in his ministry of the Scriptures that they did not have (John 7:40-52); and response from and popularity among the people that they certainly had never known (Mark 12:37). They could have allowed the gracious Spirit of God to lead their thinking and feeling so that they would have begun to understand and to come to faith, but they refused. They were bitter. They were hard. They were ruthless and they accused Jesus of being in league with the devil. You can imagine them in various places speaking contemptuously about Jesus' ministry being emotional and extreme, and doing their best to keep people from going to hear Jesus preach. There are none so bitter against authentic, Spirit-owned, biblical ministry as those who do not stand by the Scriptures and who preach only reassuring platitudes. Jesus spoke plainly and so did Paul (Acts 20:20,26-31). Perhaps the only people more bitter against thoroughgoing ministry than unbelievers are converted people who have backslidden, and who no longer stand and live by the gospel that first constrained them to profess faith unto salvation. Never be taken aback or distracted by bitter criticism.

The devil exposed

Read also Luke 4:1-13

Jesus stated in the clearest terms that their comments were utterly stupid. They were so blinded by their hatred that they no longer talked sense. How could it be true that Satan would cast out his own agents and demolish his own king-dom? Jesus, while recognizing that there is an organized kingdom of evil, was not suggesting that that kingdom is a harmonious unity. One of the many comforting things that emerge from the Book of Revelation is that there are ten-sions and destructive confusions within the armies and agents of Satan (Rev. 17:15-18). There are times when the 'kings of the earth' come together against God and the gospel, only to discover that their power is minimal compared to that of God (Ps. 2:1-11). Jesus explained his power over the agents and activities of evil in vivid pictorial terms. He is the strong man who has entered the world arena of Satan's territory and has demonstrated his victorious power. That had been made clear in the comprehensive confrontation of the temptation (Luke 4:1-13) and would, in due time, be sealed finally in the death and resurrection of the Saviour. By virtue of his victory, Jesus can and does deliver those held in Satan's power. Put in the simplest of terms: Jesus is stronger than Satan. There is a wonderful picture here of the work of the gospel. Men and women held in Satan's power are being set free. Little wonder Satan resists with great anger. We need to be aware of this, not least when the church gathers for prayer. *We* do not bind Satan. That is Jesus' work. But, in faith, we claim that victory so that the word of the gospel may run free to bring salvation to many (Eph. 6:18-19; Col. 4:3; 2 Thess. 3:1).

The unpardonable sin

Read also 1 John 1:7 - 2:2

These solemn verses must be read carefully in order to avoid the terrible distress and fear they have caused to many. Note first the glorious affirmation that *all* manner of sins and blasphemies will be forgiven. What a gospel message to all who feel they have failed and blundered terribly into sin and shame! There is full forgiveness and cleansing for all who confess their sins. Read 1 John 1:7 - 2:2; Isaiah 1:18; Jeremiah 31:34, and let your heart rejoice. Those who fear they have committed the unpardonable sin need to be told that the very fact that they worry about it is proof that they have not. Jesus' words here are addressed to those described in verse 30. The people who had said Jesus was in league with the devil had looked at Jesus' person. They had listened to Jesus' words. They had seen Jesus' power to heal and to save. In that context we can be sure that God the Holy Spirit had been testifying powerfully that this was indeed the Son of God, sent from God to be the Saviour of sinners. But these men, with all their religious background in the Scriptures of the Old Testament, which testify to Jesus Christ (as Luke 24:25-27,44-48 make plain), denied the person of Jesus, denied his divinity, and denied that his power had its source in God. They said that everything concerning Jesus was inspired by the devil. That is the kind of sin that costs a man his soul and sends him to a lost eternity. The unpardonable sin, the sin against the Holy Spirit, is not some single act, but a chosen, settled, defiant attitude of unbelief that refuses every gracious constraint of the Word and the Spirit, and refuses to yield to Jesus. When a man or woman looks at love incarnate and does not want it, but persists in hating it, then for that person there is no more hope of forgiveness. That is indeed solemn.

Real family bonds

Read also Ephesians 2:11-22

Jesus' relatives had gone out to take charge of him because they thought he had been 'carried away' by his enthusiasm for and commitment to what he saw as God's calling for him (v. 21). Now we see the family arriving where Jesus was and, because they could not get near for the crowd, they sent in a message. Jesus took this opportunity to teach an important lesson. We must not think that Jesus was denying and devaluing family love, loyalty and respect. He would never have repudiated the commandment to honour father and mother (Exod. 20:12). Nor must we read too much into the fact that the family group was 'outside', although they did not at this stage recognize or respond to his ministry. Mary and the others may well have had a measure of faith (Luke 2:19) but were allowing human considerations and care to narrow their commitment to service. Think how Christian parents sometimes hold back their children from the ministry or missionary service because they see it as too costly. Jesus makes plain that there is a greater loyalty than that of family. To do the will of God comes first (Luke 2:49). This forges a deeper bond than mere flesh and blood relationship. There is a family fellowship, a sense of belonging and sharing, that is found only in the life of faith and obedience. Of course, those who find in Christ and in the fellowship of his people such reassuring love, care and support will long that their family relatives may be drawn in to share it. Remember that, in the midst of his agony on the cross, Jesus made sure his mother was cared for. Mary could have had no doubt about the love of her Son and the value he set on her (John 19:25-27). We too can be part of God's family, built together and belonging together, which is life and blessing indeed (Eph. 2:11-13,19-22).

The sower and the seed

Read also Isaiah 55:6-11

The crowd listening to Jesus was a very mixed one, just like the average Sunday congregation. Gathered by the sea there would have been the enthusiasts who followed Jesus everywhere, the casual passers-by, the main body of disciples already in some measure committed to Jesus, and also those who would be at various stages of understanding and response. All of them would recognize the picture of the farmer sowing seed but Jesus did not assume that all would hear with understanding, let alone with faith (v. 9). Even the disciples seem to have 'missed the point' of the parable (v. 13) and there is a lesson here for all who preach and teach, especially among the young. Illustrations are useful only if they do illustrate, brighten and show clearly the truth that is being taught. There is a particular danger in 'children's addresses' just as there is in 'dramatic presentations' because the 'show' can be enjoyed without the spiritual message being grasped at all. Think again of the variety of people in the crowd. Jesus was seeking to reach them all: to cause some to wonder if the seed of the Word was taking root in them; to cause others to realize that things in their lives were working against the good God sought to do for them; and to cause the disciples to learn that there would be significant 'wastage' and that they should not therefore be discouraged. Jesus had total confidence in what he was teaching. He was confident that in and through the preaching of God's truth, God's work is done, and not all preachers are like that (Isa. 55:10-11; Rom. 10:17). Jesus made no emotional appeal, as verse 9 makes plain. It is the work of the Holy Spirit to apply the Word and he does so, sometimes with immediate effect and sometimes over a long process of time, as in the germination of a seed.

It makes you think!

Read also Ephesians 2:1-9

These are difficult verses. Jesus states plainly that it had been given to the believing disciples to know and to grasp the 'secret' (the mystery revealed) of the kingdom. The gospel of salvation is not something people could ever work out for themselves. It is beyond human understanding that God should send his eternal Son to become man, and to die for sinners, as their substitute, to pay the price of sin. Only the gracious, effective work of the Holy Spirit can open eyes and hearts to see and believe the truth. Salvation is God's work, a sovereign enabling whereby those dead in sin can hear and believe (Eph. 2:1-8; John 5:25). But what of those who do not see and do not believe? On the face of it Jesus seems to say that he taught the crowds with the specific purpose of keeping them in the dark. But taking the words 'so that' (v. 12) in an unqualified way contradicts the whole purpose of the gospel, which speaks of Jesus as the Light that shows the way to God. Jesus' words in verse 12 are quoted from Isaiah 6:9-10 where the prophet is recounting his call to the ministry and reviewing its course and outcome. As he spoke God's Word to the people it seemed only to have the effect of hardening their hearts. There has always been a mystery about why some believe and some do not, and in trying to understand this we must keep to the clear statements of Scripture, accepting that some things must remain in the secret counsel of God's sovereign providence. When baffled we say in faith, 'Will not the Judge of all the earth do right?' (Gen. 18:25).

Listen well!

Read also Hebrews 3:7-13

Mark's words should make it plain that nothing remains static. When God's Word is being preached and heard, things are happening. For some, the truth becomes crystal clear, and for others, both mind and heart become increasingly blind and hard. The parables we are about to study are set in the context of a ministry that had already gone on a considerable time with many indications and proofs of God's authentication. But while there had been great general response there had also been significant unbelief and resistance, hardening into deliberate rejection. Paul speaks of this twofold result of the preaching of the gospel in 2 Corinthians 2:15-16, stressing that, right from the time some hear the gospel, the process of hardening begins in a way that is never reversed. Perhaps the key to these verses is the fact that Jesus did not use blinding revelations and works of power to overcome people. These 'wrong roads to the kingdom' were rejected in the temptation (Matt. 4:1-11). Having the senses overcome and stunned is not the same as being brought to faith. The parables presented truth in a form that unveiled the truth to faith that reached out, and veiled the truth to unbelief that refused it. Little wonder Jesus warned people to take heed *how* they heard. Neither preaching nor listening is a game or an entertainment. It is life and death. Read Paul's solemn words in Romans 1:19-23, and take heed lest you have an unbelieving heart.

A parable explained

Read also Romans 10:8-15

A farmer sowing his seed by hand would have been a familiar sight to the people listening to Jesus. There is no suggestion of any defect in the method of the sower nor in the seed he used. The seed sown is the Word of God, and apart from that we have nothing to sow that has any hope of producing a good result. We are not in the entertainment, amusement or popularity business. Sowing good seed is work: hard, ongoing work that includes preparation, ploughing, weeding and waiting. It also calls for faith, because unless we have confidence in what is being sown we will very soon give up and turn to other pursuits. The seed of the Word has life and power within itself and, once it is sown, we must not interfere with it, save only to water the seed with prayer. We must pray for the preaching of the Word, and for the guarding of the seed of the Word once it is preached. Wherever the good seed is being sown Satan seeks to frustrate the whole process. We must be careful lest the tramping traffic of our worldly lives makes our hearts impervious to the Word. Sometimes there will be a quick, enthusiastic response to the Word, but when the real business of ongoing discipleship and the demands of duty begin to lay claim to time and energy, the enthusiasm fades and converts fall away. The seed landing among thorns has a fight from the beginning. The farmer may have cleared the ground but the roots of thorns go deep. Jesus makes it clear that the problem is simply the overcrowded lives of the people who received the seed of the Word. Career as well as pleasure and enjoyment can choke spiritual life and draw the heart away from the Lord Jesus. We need the warning of 1 Peter 2:11 about things that wage war against our souls!

The parable summed up

Read also Matthew 13:24-30; 1 Corinthians 3:5-9

The first lot of seed was snatched away by the devil; the second found only a shallow, superficial hold on life; the third fought to keep the place it had claimed in life but found the crowded situation too much for it. How important it is for a Christian to keep the garden of the heart and life weed-free and well watered. Just as there are garden pests so there are spiritual ones. Some pests are hidden and attack the roots, and friends may wonder why some Christians are making no progress at all. There may be secret sins or secret hurts, disappointments and personality struggles that need to be brought to Jesus to be dealt with. Jesus teaches that, in spite of all the failures and disappointments, the final quarter of the seed produces such a bountiful but varied harvest that there is cause for rejoicing. This is a confirmation of the glorious statement in Isaiah 55:11. God's Word accomplishes what it was sent to do in his sovereign will and purpose, and our labour in the Lord is not in vain (1 Cor. 15:58), no matter what it may seem to be at any interim stage. In our given work, which may be clearing the ground preparatory to ploughing, or the actual sowing of the seed, or the energetic privilege of gathering in the harvest, we must never forget that it is God alone who gives the increase (1 Cor. 3:5-8). The triumph is his, and so are the praise and the glory. It is instructive to remember that at this point Matthew gives the parable of the weeds and the wheat, which tells of the secret activity of the enemy, the panic of the servants when the evil became evident, and the quiet calm assurance of the Master. Not even the full operation of evil right to harvest time can frustrate the final harvest (Matt. 13:24-30).

A lamp on a stand

Read also 1 Peter 1:22 - 2:3

Jesus now speaks of the Word, not as seed, but as light which shines to make everything manifest or exposed. God's Word is a lamp and a light (Ps. 119:105; Prov. 6:20-23). It makes us wise unto salvation (2 Tim. 3:15) and nourishes us in our growth in grace (1 Peter 1:22 - 2:3). But Scripture also affirms that Jesus is light, and his light was resented, for obvious reasons (John 3:19). Jesus also said that those who follow him will not walk in darkness but will have the light of life (John 8:12). A Christian is really someone who is lit up by Jesus and called to let that light, which is Jesus' light, shine in an unshadowed way wherever we happen to be (Matt. 5:16; Phil. 2:15). Light does not have to try to be fireworks! A steady light is what counts, and all we have to do is to keep the windows of our life clean and the light will shine. As we learn from Jesus, and as we become more naturally trusting in him, we will bear testimony to him in all sorts of ways and, at the right times, by word of mouth. Of course, light will always reveal what is false, in ourselves and in others. But it is as we learn to walk in the light, out in the open with God (and *wisely* open with others) that we begin to enjoy the kind of fellowship that brings health to our lives and a healing influence on all with whom we come in contact. The emphasis in these verses is certainly that the light we have been given is to be shared with others. But another aspect of light is that Jesus shines the light of understanding into our private thinking so that we can begin to understand ourselves and, by his grace, begin to handle ourselves more wisely, to the benefit of all.

Listen carefully

Read also Psalm 19:7-14

Jesus speaks of the Word as a message to be heard, which, when taken to heart, exercises a moulding effect on the personality and life. He also emphasizes that we must be very careful what we hear (v. 24). In Luke 8:16-18 Jesus says we must be careful how we listen. It is a serious business when God speaks to us and that is why we must come to church expecting to meet with God and to hear his voice. Both exhortations, what and how, are important. There is so much in the media that we should neither see nor hear. With the proliferation of radio, tapes and television, we are rarely without some kind of sight or sound around us. We are often neither listening intelligently nor giving our full attention to what we are doing. We learn the habit of being casual in our attention, and automatic in our responses, with the result that we give the same kind of half attention to those around us. This leads to a society of indifference. The same attitude of casual involvement is transferred to our church life, and our daily Bible reading. If our dealings with God are characterized by such divided attention we can become the kind of Christians who always *mean* to do certain things; but we all know where the road of good intentions can lead! Jesus urges his followers to be in earnest, because the measure of single-heartedness they give will be the measure of blessing they will have in return. If we shut ourselves in (whether because of fear or guilt or a sense of inferiority) we will shut ourselves out from a richness of sweet, strong fellowship that the Lord longs for his people. We do not need our fears, guilt or sense of inferiority, because we are chosen of God in Christ. We are accepted in him. As you listen to the good Word of God, see that you respond in faith and obedience. That is how life is enriched.

A word of encouragement

Read also 1 Corinthians 4:1-5

In the work of God's kingdom it is easy to be disheartened by circumstances and difficulties and so be disappointed in the results of our work. Think of the 'failures' in the parable of the seed and the sower. In describing the seed growing secretly, slowly and surely, Jesus means to encourage us and give us confidence in his providential care. The seasons pass, the farmer's activity changes, and at times the only thing he can do is to wait. We are dealing here with the slow growth of the seed, which has life in itself and which, in response to various influences, develops and ripens. In a garden, green shoots push through even ground hard with frost. Then in due time, although we may consider that there has been too much or too little rain, too much or too little or too late sunshine, the harvest comes. Just as in the natural realm, so it is in the spiritual realm. We must not interfere with God's processes. The seed of the Word develops according to laws of its own being and nature. In different soils, that is, in different lives, the seed grows at different speeds and we should not judge any situation before the right time (1 Cor. 4:1-5). It is significant that the illustration used is agricultural. In the work of the gospel, whether in evangelism or in building churches, we are in the business of growth, not explosions! It is easy to create a big bang and impress people, even Christians. But after the bang, when the dust has settled, what is there of permanence? Real life takes time to grow; but it *will* grow to spiritual maturity, stability and service. God's labourers need a lot of patience in the back-breaking and sometimes heart-breaking toil, always ploughing and preparing new ground, always weeding and guarding the field, always sowing the seed. Be encouraged. God is at work.

Astonishing growth

Read also 1 Corinthians 1:18-31

This parable emphasizes the contrast between the smallness of the seed and the vastness of the result. Even in modern Israel you can see that wherever there is a crack in a wall or pavement, with a scrap of soil, the mustard seed will take root and grow. In due time the mustard pods ripen and burst and the scattered seeds, so small that they are carried far by the wind, take root and the process begins all over again. In the church we are all too concerned with size, numbers and with measurable growth. Statistics can so easily become a form of idolatry, not least in that they focus our attention on what *we* are doing, and we can be led into the snare of comparing our own work with that of others, hoping to prove that we are better than they. But the work is not ours. It is God alone who gives the increase (1 Cor. 3:5-8). In any case, since the seed is scattered far and wide, we are never in a position to make any authentic calculation about what we have actually accomplished. But there is encouragement here, not just searching correction. It is easy to despise the day of small things (Zech. 4:10). For example, we look at the powers of the world and the surging political movements and, in comparison, the church of Jesus Christ looks small, weak, ignored and beleaguered. We look at Bethlehem and all we see is a helpless child. We look at the cross and it seems a picture of total weakness. But it was that despised and rejected Jesus who broke the power of sin, death and hell, and it was in his victory that the servants of Jesus turned the world upside down. Ponder well Paul's words in 1 Corinthians 1:18-31. The weakness of God proved to be mightily strong. It had been promised from the beginning of time that a 'seed' from God would come (Gen. 3:15, AV), the Saviour that sinners needed.

Private tuition

Read also Mark 15:6-15

There are important lessons in these brief verses for all whose business it is in any way to teach God's Word, particularly those who feel drawn to an aggressive form of evangelism in which every session of preaching is made an occasion of direct, deliberate confrontation and appeal for 'decision'. Decisions have to be made. People must either follow Jesus or crucify him (Mark 15:6-15). But we must take into account how little many people know about God, Jesus and the Bible. Their ignorance can be almost total. We must also allow for the religious confusion of many due to the defective and false teaching they have had since childhood. There are many who think that, because they were baptized as babies, they will go to heaven. We must also allow for people's complicated lives and personalities and for the different stages they are at in their understanding and in their ability to grasp more truth. We are told that Jesus adapted his methods, though not his message, to their capacity. With vivid parables, easy to understand on one level, he held their attention, kindled their curiosity, sharpened their enquiry and, as they were able, he led them into the truth. Jesus did not force a response from people before they were able to understand what they were responding and committing themselves to, or refusing. Some thought their long years of religion meant they were better than others, but the parables, and their inability to grasp them, revealed their spiritual poverty. Think of the various ways Jesus dealt with individuals. What a wise evangelist and counsellor he was! He did not trample over people's feelings. A true shepherd never harasses his sheep. He values them too highly. Note, lastly, the patience Jesus had with his disciples, explaining things over and over again (cf. Phil. 3:1).

A lesson in faith

Read also Psalm 46:1-11

Jesus taught his disciples faith not only by parables but also through the experiences into which he led them. It was Jesus' decision to cross the Sea of Galilee and the disciples did not hesitate. The phrase 'they took him' seems to indicate that they were aware of his deep weariness after the long session of teaching the crowd. To begin with everything was 'normal' and the sight of Jesus asleep in the stern of the boat would have given them all a sense of well-being, and even pleasure, because they were 'doing something' for their Master. But we must recognize that following Jesus in obedient service can at times lead to storms. When the storm raged, the disciples' attention was fixed on the wind, the waves and the boat taking in water. Jesus sleeping serenely was no longer a source of peace but a cause for alarm. They assumed that he was at the mercy of the elements, just as they felt they were, and in blind panic they forgot all they had learned, and accused him of not caring that they were about to perish. The disciples had faith, assurance and confidence when the sea was calm. But such was their panic, that surely this was no ordinary storm. They were heading for Gadara and for a work of mighty deliverance in a life held captive by the power of sin, and this storm could be seen as Satan's attempt to prevent their arrival. It was certainly an assault on the disciples' faith. Of course, if there had been any real danger Jesus would not have been asleep. When they woke him, he refused to be rushed by their panic. He calmed the storm and then spoke to them about their fear and lack of faith. The miracle was a concession to the weakness of the disciples' faith. Had they trusted, they would have ridden the storm, and their faith would have been stronger in the end.

Who is this Jesus?

Read also Luke 9:7-9,18-20

The disciples were filled with awe and said to each other,
'Who is this?' It is good when we take time to consider just
who Jesus is. This same question was asked by the evil
King Herod in Luke 9:7-9. The Pharisees asked it in Luke
5:21. Jesus himself posed the question to the disciples in
Luke 9:18-20. We have the same kind of questioning about
the person of Jesus in Matthew 13:53-57; John 6:41-42; and
Matthew 21:9-11. 'Who then is this?' is a fundamental and
vital question and the answer will set the direction of our
lives. This was the question Paul asked on the Damascus
road in Acts 9:1-5, and the realization of the answer trans-
formed his life and made him a mighty servant of God. The
disciples asked the question here, because the stilling of
the wind and waves had caused a storm of perplexity and
disturbance in their minds and hearts. They had grown
accustomed to Jesus, thinking of him as a man just like
themselves. Of course, Jesus really was and is one of us in
a very real sense, because he freely and gladly took our
human nature to share our life and experience. Hebrews
2:9-10,17-18; 4:14-16; Philippians 2:5-8; and John 1:14 and
many other Scriptures make this plain. But he is not just
one of us. He is the eternal Word, the Son of God, by whom
all things were made and by whom all things hold together
(John 1:1-3; Col. 1:15-20; Heb. 1:1-3). This Jesus is none
other than the Lord of Glory (1 Cor. 2:8), the Lord of Creation. When we once see his glory we are not surprised by
the authority of his word nor by his acts of sovereign power.
'The waves and wind still know his voice who ruled them
while he dwelt below' (from the hymn 'Be still my soul' by
Katherina von Schlegel). As he lay sleeping he seemed so
ordinary. But faith should see beyond the ordinary.

Terror in society

Read also Luke 11:17-26

This is the story of the stilling of a frightening storm in a man's life. We must not be distracted by what happened to the pigs. We seldom have qualms about having bacon and egg for breakfast! It may have been that Jesus gave permission for the evil spirits to go into the pigs as the most effective and obvious way of conveying to the man that he had indeed been delivered. If this area was Jewish, why had they such herds of swine, which were forbidden by their own law? If this was a community living in conscious disregard of God's laws, then it is not surprising that some of the younger generation were finding their lives dominated by the powers of evil. Perhaps the older generation, still with remnants of godly religion from their forefathers, had not slid into such obvious evil. They may have simply settled for the idolatry of obsessive materialism, as we shall see in verse 16. But the powers of evil, given the opportunity when society forgets God, are quick to move in. That the man was in the grip of evil spirits is beyond question. That his whole personality was taken over is clear from the facts recorded. Jesus seems to have addressed one evil spirit (v. 8), but then a multiplicity of evil spirits is indicated in verse 9. The specific number of the stampeding herd (v. 13) does not mean that that number of evil spirits possessed the man. But we have here a vivid reminder that evil is real, that its agents and agencies are many, and that if given the chance, their power to invade human life is strong. As we consider the many frightening happenings in contemporary society we need to ask why such things should be; and recognize that evil can be more than just human badness. There is a devil, and his capacity to destroy human lives is real. A Saviour is needed.

My name is Legion

Read also Romans 6:16-23

One of the solemn aspects of this story is that we have simply no idea how this man's life became so totally dominated by evil. Matthew 8:28 speaks of two demon-possessed men and there may even have been a gang of them. Had they trifled with evil: sex, sorcery, drugs, indulgence, so that some of them became trapped? No doubt the man never meant his life to end up like this. He may have had regrets, remorse, or he may still have been rebellious. Certainly he was beyond the control of society and beyond self-control. His life was marked by wildness, isolation, darkness, loneliness, suffering and fear. He was withdrawn, a drop-out, with a grotesque lifestyle among the darkness and the graves. If we knew what had started him on this road we could set a guard for ourselves. We need to be careful. Risks can prove very costly. There are things and a way of life that wage war against the soul, the personality and the life (1 Peter 2:11). Whatever else this man was, he was not free. The amazing thing is that the presence of Jesus had the double effect of first drawing the man and almost at the same time causing him to shout words of fierce rejection. When Jesus asked his name it was an act of care, which brought him back to a sense of his identity, humanity and value. No one had spoken to him like that for a long time. In the eyes of society he was useless and worthless. But it was not Jesus' kindness that solved the man's problem and set him free to live a new life. This was the Jesus who had come to bring salvation by virtue of his death and resurrection. This is the Jesus who is able to save to the uttermost (Heb. 7:25, AV). For this man it meant forgiveness. It meant the breaking of the power of cancelled sin. It meant freedom from Satan's dominion. That is salvation.

The prejudice of unbelief

Read also Hebrews 2:1-3; 4:1-2

The herdsmen did not seem to be interested in what Jesus had done for the man, because they fled. Perhaps their only concern was the possibility of losing their jobs because of the loss of the pigs. When the people came to see what had happened, they saw this well-known young outcast sitting clothed and in his right mind, listening to Jesus, and enjoying every minute of it; and their reaction was fear. They had been afraid of the man when he was wild and now they feared him when he was quiet. They do not seem to have enquired about the change. Perhaps they had heard about Jesus and had already decided that they did not want this kind of enthusiastic religion in their community, because it would change things. Perhaps they had decided that if they, and their 'social services', could do nothing with this kind of man, then no one else could. Jesus could, and did, but it was beyond their understanding so they did not like it. They preferred things the way they had always been, even if the new was better. That is what is known as prejudice. Then the herdsmen told about the encounter with the man and also about the pigs. That settled it. If powerful religion was going to bring financial loss and an economic slump, then religion had to go. They began to beg Jesus to go away. Note the intensity and eagerness. It could not happen quickly enough. For all we know there may have been even more pigs nearer the town, and perhaps even more social drop-outs. If Jesus intended to go on into their town the possibility of economic disaster was immense. It is quite amazing what different people actually see when they hear Jesus and witness his power to save and transform human lives. They begged Jesus to go, and he went. That is solemn indeed.

Light in a dark place

Read also Matthew 5:14-16; Ephesians 5:1-16

The citizens were not the only ones to plead earnestly with Jesus. The man, who knew what Jesus had done for him, who had sat and listened to Jesus' gracious words, and who already knew the love that Jesus had for him, begged to join the band of disciples and go with them. Perhaps he just wanted to get away from the place and the people where his life had been virtually destroyed. He was more aware than most of just how dominant were the powers of evil and he wanted to have nothing more to do with the place. If only we all learned to keep away from people and places that will do nothing but harm to our Christian lives and service! Perhaps he wanted to do something for this Jesus who had done so much for him. But he assumed serving Jesus meant 'full time' with the disciples: in the ministry, or on the mission-field. Of course God does call people to that kind of service. But that was not the way for this man. His service was going to be more challenging and more demanding. Jesus told him to go back to the community and to the people who knew him best, to show them by his changed life and by his spoken testimony how much the Lord had done for him. The man obeyed, and people marvelled. No doubt some said it would not last. Others would wait for the man to return to his old ways. But it did not happen. It must have been a very lonely life for that young believer, but Jesus, the great Intercessor, would pray for him. He who worked this great transformation is the same yesterday and today and for ever (Heb. 13:8). His touch still has its ancient power. But he needs witnesses. Light has to be present in dark places if needy people are to see it. If unbelievers have no contact with Christians, how are they to hear about Jesus and his power to save and give life?

A last resort

Read also Luke 8:40-48

The stories of two very different people are mingled together. Both people faced a storm of fear, anxiety and disappointment. Jesus had returned to the highly populated side of the Sea of Galilee and was again surrounded by a crowd. At first the focus is on one man. Jairus, a ruler of the synagogue, was drawn to Jesus, just like the wild man of Gadara, by a need that he felt so deeply. Rulers of the synagogue were not normally found near Jesus except in a critical spirit, but this man publicly knelt before him, declared his daughter's death was imminent, and begged Jesus to come and heal her. Jesus at once fell into step with Jairus and went with him. Read Luke 8:40-48 to see the emphasis on twelve years in the case of both Jairus and the sick woman. In one case they were years of happy family life, now shattered by crisis, and in the other case years of debilitating, demoralizing sickness. Both had the effect of compelling two very different people to seek help from Jesus. In each case Jesus was a last desperate hope. We know little about the woman. Was she old or young, married or single? Perhaps she was lonely and bitter because her particular sickness caused her to be regarded as 'unclean' and thus barred from the synagogue (Lev. 15:25-30). She had heard about Jesus (v. 27), but we do not know how, perhaps from a friend. We do not know why she had not sought help sooner. Sometimes it is only when we are at the end of our tether that we seek out Jesus. Now it was all or nothing.

Come to me

Read also Matthew 11:28-30

We need to keep in mind that some people are so hurt by life's experiences that they need help and encouragement to come to Jesus. This woman's 'faith' seems to have included a measure of superstition, and the touching of his garment may have been wishful thinking. On the other hand, her tentative faith may have been totally genuine but untaught. She came secretly, fearing that she might be rejected. The moment she touched the hem of Jesus' garment he knew; and she knew that she had been healed. No one else knew. The woman could have slipped away into the crowd to be an anonymous, secret disciple, probably still lonely, friendless and without acceptance in society or church. Jesus called her into the open to enable her both to confirm her faith by confessing it, and also to hear the wonderfully gracious and tender words spoken by him in such a personal caring way. Up to this point she had heard about Jesus, had known of his power to heal, but now she met him face to face. She was no longer just a statistic listed among the needy in society. She was a real person. Jesus had given her back not only her health, but her life, her dignity, her hope; and he sent her on her way with his peace. If there is one lesson we learn from this story it is that we should never hesitate to come to Jesus. Remember this when next we sing in church:

> There is no place where earth's sorrows
> Are more felt than up in heaven;
> There is no place where earth's failings
> Have such kindly judgment given.

(F. W. Faber)

Why does God delay?

Read also Psalm 31:1-5,14-15; Psalm 37:1-7

One person must have been exasperated and even hurt by the incident with the woman. Put yourself in Jairus' position. He had come to Jesus first. His daughter was at the point of death. This woman's case could have been dealt with by Jesus later, assuming, of course, that her courage had held out. But Jesus is never hesitant or uncertain. Just as establishing the woman's faith was more important than healing her body, so confirming Jairus' faith was Jesus' first concern. Jesus cared about the woman's health, the child's serious illness and Jairus' distress. He always does care, but he often sees greater needs and deeper issues that lead to greater blessing long term. The news of the daughter's death was broken with what seems unnecessary bluntness and even criticism of Jesus for not acting sooner. (He did not need to go in person to perform the miracle as Matthew 8:5-13 makes plain.) At that precise point, Jesus said, 'Do not fear, only believe.' The appeal, or command, was simply, 'Trust me.' Note the wisdom and care shown by Jesus in allowing only Peter, James and John to accompany him. When they came to the house, Jairus' wife may well have had a look of rebuke on her face as if to say, 'Why have you been so long?' But in the face of death Jesus was calm and assured. He was the victor. Met by the scorn of the official mourners, Jesus had no hesitation. He put them out. Mocking unbelief never sees the power of God. The miracle was done with utmost gentleness and care so as not to frighten anyone, especially the one who heard the words, 'Little girl, get up.' Jesus gave her back to her parents, insisting that all should be normal. The first thing the girl saw was her parents standing with Jesus. That is the best thing we can ever give to our children.

The carpenter?

Read also Luke 4:14-30

Jesus returned to his home town of Nazareth, where he had lived for thirty years (Luke 2:51-52). He and his family were well known there, as were his ministry and miracles performed in other places. The first reaction of the congregation in the synagogue was that they were astonished at his wisdom, but this soon turned to annoyance and they took offence. It is an attitude still found in congregations: 'Who does he think he is, preaching to us like that?' They recognized Jesus as the young fellow who had grown up among them, but they did not recognize him as the man sent from God, nor did they recognize the grace and truth from God that were in his words. They were more at ease with their own dull, dead forms of religion and neither expected nor desired a living message from God. Luke 4:14-30 records the same incident more fully. It is clear that, even as he preached, Jesus was aware of the cynicism regarding himself, the resentment at, and the refusal of, his message. No doubt feeling the human hurt of their attitude, Jesus said graciously but firmly that a prophet is not likely to be recognized in his home community nor in his family. The other three Gospels, written later, omit the reference to Jesus' family, possibly because by that time more of his family had in fact believed on him (John 7:5; 1 Cor. 15:7; Gal. 1:19). Could the rejection of Jesus in Nazareth be in part due to the strange but deep-seated jealousy in human nature that does not like to see 'one of our own' excelling, or making greater progress than ourselves? Jealousy is an evil to be guarded against.

Unbelief affects others

Read also Revelation 2:8-16

It is a solemn thought that the sovereign, saving power of God in Jesus Christ can be restricted and even cancelled out by human unbelief. Matthew 13:58 states that Jesus deliberately refused to do mighty works in Nazareth because of their attitude of unbelief. 'The point is, not that Jesus was powerless apart from men's faith, but that in the absence of faith, he could not work mighty works in accordance with the purpose of his ministry. For to have worked miracles where faith was absent would, in most cases anyway, have been merely to have aggravated men's guilt and hardened them against God' (C. E. B. Cranfield). This is seen again with the unbelieving Pharisees who demanded signs and miracles as a condition for their believing in him (Matt. 12:38-42). Mark's reference to a few being healed may indicate that some had the first flickering of faith, or that Jesus, in his mighty compassion, chose to act for those who were being 'suffocated' by the unbelief of the community. There are still areas of society where unbelief is so established and powerful that we are wise, in the interest of our soul's salvation and growth in grace, to keep away from them, unless God has specifically called us to serve there. There are also 'congregations' that are so much citadels of gospel-denying attitudes (Rev. 2:9 calls them 'synagogues of Satan') that true believers may put their souls in peril by remaining in them. Jesus was amazed at the unbelief in Nazareth. These people, who had known him all these years, and who had experienced incarnate truth, grace and love living amongst them in their everyday lives, had not just been unaware of it and unmoved by it, they had refused it. Little wonder we are warned that an evil heart of unbelief leads us away from God (Heb. 3:12).

Uncluttered lives

Read also Matthew 9:35 - 10:1

Jesus' reaction to established unbelief was to send out his disciples in a work of evangelism. Matthew 9:35 - 10:1 shows us that this was due to Jesus' compassion for people, who were like sheep without a shepherd. When we study this passage we must be careful because some enthusiasts tend to focus on authority over evil spirits rather than on the call to repentance (v. 12). But if we are to emphasize verses 7 and 13 to make them vital elements in gospel ministry, we must in honesty give equal emphasis to verses 8-9, which speak of radical self-denial in areas of food, money and dress. Note also the reference in verse 6 to Jesus going to the villages, the less populated, less promising and less privileged places. This seems to be the example he was setting to these commissioned and 'empowered' disciples. The Twelve were sent to people who knew little or nothing about the gospel and it was among such as these that they were to preach, teach, break the power of evil in human lives, and bring healing to sick bodies and personalities. Remember that Judas Iscariot was among the Twelve. He would do the same as the others. Would people believe and would evil spirits yield to his ministry? Read Matthew 7:21-23 and remember that not all who say the right things and perform 'signs and wonders' are necessarily God's workers. In our day, when there are so many false prophets and antichrists (1 John 2:18; 4:1), we need to consider carefully the actions of some who claim to be messengers of God with power from on high. Very often they do not operate among the unchurched and unreached, such as those to whom the Twelve were sent, but like 'sheep-stealers' (John 10:1,10-13) they prey on vulnerable and insecure Christians who already belong to the evangelical community.

Lessons for service

Read also John 15:1-8

There are many lessons about Christian service here. Jesus first called his men to himself: all fruitful service begins and continues in our submission to and fellowship with Jesus (John 15:1-8). The disciples were sent out two by two, for mutual encouragement and caution. There is danger in being a 'loner', because, having no one to consult, we can assume infallibility. Always remember that we can be wrong! In ministry and in missionary service we need to recognize the need to maintain true contact with our home base. But what of those Christians who have never actually joined a church or those who, having joined, have refused to become part of the regular prayer-life of their own congregation? Too many who never share in prayer want to be prayed for when they set out in service. There is something wrong in that attitude! The exhortation in verses 8-9, although relating to life then, seems to call for a lifestyle that is essentially simple and uncluttered, detached as far as is practical from many things and activities that devour our best time and energy. Many congregations and Christian organizations so multiply activities and involvements that their main calling and witness tend to get sidelined. Verses 10-11 do not suggest that we impose on people for hospitality and support, but remind us that in Christian service we will meet rejection as well as acceptance. There are times when we must recognize rejection and turn away from the situation rather than labour futilely against it. Such an action may even be used by God to awaken people to the seriousness of their condition. One constant danger is that *we* are accepted but our message is refused. It is easy to compromise, giving people the impression that, because they like us and we accept them, they are right with God.

An evil man

Read also Luke 3:1-6,15-20

At first sight, the ugly story of Herod seems to break into the ongoing ministry of Jesus and the disciples, but it is in fact an illustration of what the servants of the gospel may meet if faithful in their witness. If part of the message of the gospel is a call to repent (v. 12), it means that those who hear will be challenged about the wrong in their lives. That challenge may well be resisted, even if people's consciences are convicted, and that is exactly what happened in the case of Herod. This man, son of the Herod who slaughtered the children at the time of Jesus' birth (Matt. 2:16), was, humanly speaking, a brilliant man, sly as a fox, as Jesus described him (Luke 13:32), cruel, sensual and indulgent, as his personal life made plain. Herodias was his brother's wife and Herod stole her for himself. John the Baptist, a fearless preacher of righteousness, had rebuked Herod, perhaps on some public occasion of preaching, and the king's resentment led first to his arrest and then to his murder. Herod's weakness is clear in verse 26 and he was afraid lest there should be any shadow on his public image. The foul execution took place just to please a wicked woman as immoral as he was. Herod the schemer had been trapped and outwitted by his wife, who had nursed her grudge against John and had waited her opportunity. Of course, Herod fell into the trap much earlier when, troubled in conscience by John's ministry and knowing him to be a righteous man sent from God, he tried to evade the issue. Perhaps he imprisoned John to keep him out of the clutches of his vengeful wife, perhaps because he feared public reaction if he harmed John. Herod hesitated, and he was lost. Compromise seldom works. When we make, or evade, a decision, we should consider the long-term consequences.

Evading God

Read also 1 Corinthians 6:9-11

Herod's past had caught up with him and he was afraid. God had been speaking to him through John the Baptist long before news of Jesus' ministry began to reach him. The focus of the challenge was, as it so often is, a wrong relationship: one that should never have begun and one Herod refused to put right. Now the ministry of Jesus and the Twelve was expanding and Herod heard about it. Without question, the power of God attended this ministry, but it is amazing just how confused the reactions were (vv. 14-15). Many simply did not recognize that God himself was speaking to them and calling for a response of faith. I remember a time, years ago, when a particularly challenging sermon was preached and there was a hush of attentiveness. It was very personal. After the service a regular attender expressed how moved he had been and said, 'I had to remind myself it was just a sermon.' He did not recognize that God had been speaking to him. The confusion about Jesus, evident in these verses, continued (Mark 8:27-29). Herod was troubled, his conscience was convicted, but all he could think of was that John the Baptist's ghost had come back to trouble him. That could have reminded him of John's ministry, but it did not. His troubled conscience could have made him seek Jesus for forgiveness, but it did not. He could have recognized that once again he was in a crisis situation, with a decision to make, but, as before, he evaded the issue. Later, we are told he planned to kill Jesus as he had John (Luke 13:31). Later still, he hoped to 'discuss' things with Jesus, but Jesus had nothing to say to him (Luke 23:6-12). Perhaps the last time we were in church, we evaded the call of the gospel. Be careful. There is not a more convenient time (Acts 24:25, AV).

Time to rest

Read also Matthew 11:28-30

It is clear from the previous verses, and even clearer when we come to verses 33-34, that the ministry of Jesus and the ever-widening ministry of the Twelve was causing a great deal of interest and commotion. The Apostles returned and reported to Jesus, indicating that they knew they were his ambassadors rather than independent evangelists. No doubt they were eager to press on with the work they had been called and commissioned to do, and they may well have been surprised that Jesus insisted on their withdrawing from activity, even though they were surrounded with interest and opportunity. Of course, opportunity does not constitute a call to immediate service. Even the need does not constitute a call. Indeed, opportunity can at times become the device of the devil to cause servants of the gospel to be so endlessly active that they burn out, and life becomes a treadmill of 'fitting things in'. This is not the same as true spiritual service, and often it means, especially for ministers, that they come to their real service of preaching the Word with minds and spirits that are tired. The disciples were being taught the necessity of pacing themselves, of preparing themselves for their long-term work. Jesus was aware that his men were not nearly as ready for future service as they thought they were. Indeed, as we shall see in verse 45, the disciples were still far too influenced by what seemed immediate and large-scale success. We tend to be aware of God's good hand on our lives when he opens doors of opportunity, but we also need to be aware of his perfect handling of our lives when he closes doors and prevents our prayerful eagerness for service being fulfilled. We need to be sensitive to his leading. He acts for our blessing and our fruitfulness.

No escape!

Read also Psalm 119:9-16

The disciples had a brief time alone with Jesus on the boat but when they got to their place of retreat and rest they found an even greater crowd waiting for them. They may have felt that Jesus had been wrong in the first place. There was no possibility of rest. Jesus, moved with compassion and seeing the people's need, spent the day teaching them, and no one wanted to leave. Teaching may not have been what they expected, but Jesus knew that it is by God's Word that people find real life and hope (Matt. 4:1-4). We are not told of the disciples' reaction during the long day of teaching. We do not know if they attended carefully to what Jesus was saying. Perhaps they thought they knew it all! Perhaps they felt they were too advanced spiritually to need what 'ordinary' people needed. Perhaps they thought they would have been better off going on with their evangelism. We are told that late in the day they felt things had gone on long enough and that Jesus was forgetting the logistics of the situation. Their solution, which they thought was eminently practical, was to send the people away to fend for themselves. If, as we suggested, the disciples had not wanted quiet at the beginning, now they did, and they must have been shocked by Jesus' words in verse 37. Jesus was aware that the disciples considered themselves spiritually competent. He seems to say, 'Over to you: you meet their need.' They immediately confessed that the situation was impossible; but Jesus told them to calculate their total supply of bread. Their answer confirmed that they could see no solution. But we must never assume that Jesus is limited to our capacity. The disciples found themselves participants in a miracle. We shall see their thoughts and reactions in the next verses.

Success can be dangerous

Read also John 6:1-15

Read the whole passage from verse 30 to get the feel of the situation as well as the facts. As soon as the crowd had been fed, before any of them made a move to go home, Jesus insisted that the disciples go away in the boat. John 6:14-15 tells us that, as a result of the miraculous feeding, the crowd, in a surge of nationalistic and messianic enthusiasm, wanted to make Jesus a king. Because of this dangerous turn of events Jesus sent his disciples away from temptation. Mark, no doubt having got the facts from Peter, makes no mention of this element in the story and some commentators suggest that the crowd did not know just how miraculous their feeding had been and that only the disciples were aware of exactly what had happened. The disciples may have wanted to 'capitalize' on the miracle, to 'strike while the iron was hot' and to spread the news of the miracle and so record a great 'success'. These disciples, who had possibly not wanted to be in on this venture in the first place, who then wanted the crowd sent away, now wanted to stay with them, simply because of what they saw as a success. What their feelings were when they were dismissed with such insistence we do not know. That they were not in tune with their Master is clear, not just from the next passage, but from the fact that Jesus, having dismissed the crowd in an orderly fashion (no mean feat for one man), went into the hills to pray. Was Jesus aware again of that temptation from the devil about winning people by giving them bread (Luke 4:1-4)? It is so easy to give people what they want. Disciples are not made that way. Was Jesus burdened by the slowness of his chosen men to understand? It is so easy for us, when we think we have progressed spiritually, to be stubborn in our own opinions.

A long dark night

Read also Psalm 40:1-5,11-17

It was a long night for the disciples. What a contrast to the thrill of being involved in a miracle! It was dark; they were alone; they were distressed and no doubt afraid. Jesus too was alone, in prayer, and totally at peace. The disciples did not see Jesus, but he saw them; he saw their situation and their turmoil; yet he apparently did nothing until the fourth watch of the night. However, Jesus' inactivity and neglect of them (as they saw it) was ministering to them. They were being blessed, corrected, instructed, and prepared for their future, even though they did not know it. They were learning what they could not learn any other way. They were being taught to evaluate situations in spiritual terms rather than to react to them with immediate human emotion. All the time, in the dark, he saw them, prayed for them, and in the end he came to them. He made to go past them, walking on the water. Some try to explain this away by suggesting the boat was nearly at the shore and that Jesus was simply wading in shallow water. But many of the disciples were fishermen and they were not stupid enough to think they were in deep water when actually almost ashore! It is shocking pride to try to explain away everything that cannot be understood! Jesus came to them in the dark night of their struggle. He was about to pass by them, perhaps to wait for them when they landed; but when they cried out in obvious terror, fear having overcome faith, Jesus immediately reassured them and got into the boat. His presence brought calm to the sea but left the disciples astounded. They still had not fully understood the miraculous feeding. Their hearts were hard. How sad, after all they had been taught and had experienced. But how wonderful that at their first cry of panic Jesus was right beside them.

Jesus praying

Read also Luke 3:21-23; 6:12-16

Consider Jesus, as we are exhorted to do in Hebrews 3:1. Consider the patience he showed as he taught and prepared his chosen men for their life's calling. Consider the prayer-life of Jesus as we were told of it in verse 46. We have other references in Mark 1:35; Luke 3:21; 6:12; Mark 14:32; and Hebrews 5:7. Another significant reference to our Lord at prayer, given in Luke 9:28-29, tells us that Jesus' appearance was changed gloriously, and we may wonder if at other times in lonely prayer on the hillside the same shining of glory may have been seen. We may wonder also if in these solitary sessions Jesus may have known an agony foreshadowing Gethsemane. But there is another aspect to our Lord's prayer-life, as these words of Rev. William Still describe it: 'This is our Lord at His finest . . . His disciples being attended to, the crowd dismissed, Jesus went to the hills to keep tryst with his Father. It is beautiful. In simple terms, it is the action of the homesick son who in the evening turns to the phone-box to ring his parents and recall a little of the atmosphere of home, confide in his dear ones the happenings of the day and ask for help of one kind or another. "Is that you, Father?" "Yes, Son. What sort of day have you had, Son?" And so, the unique intimacy of Father and Son was preserved and faith strengthened, not only for another day, but for a stormy night.' It is right that we should think of our Lord Jesus Christ in the glory of his person, but we must also remember him in his true humanity. It will encourage us to speak to our heavenly Father in the open, loving, trusting way that he did. After all, Jesus is our example as well as our Saviour.

The needy are brought to Jesus

Read also Luke 18:9-14

We were told in verse 52 of the disciples' lack of under-standing and the hardness of their hearts. But why do people's hearts grow hard when they are so often in the presence of Jesus and hearing his words? Do they and we become so accustomed to hearing the good things of God that the sense of privilege diminishes? Does hardness of heart come from being too aware of ourselves, too comfortable and complacent in our position, and tending to be favourably impressed with our spirituality compared to that of others (Luke 18:9-14)? We have no idea what the disciples felt or expected when they came to land, but they must have been amazed and also challenged when they saw the eager desire of so many to bring their needy friends and neighbours to Jesus. Remember, the disciples had said of the crowd, 'Send them away and let them look after themselves' (6:35-36). There may be an echo here of the attitude that says, 'The church is there, the doors are open, we will welcome them if they come.' We may even pray that people will come. But this story is all about actually bringing people into the presence of Jesus. To do this we must speak about Jesus. We must believe that he is in fact able to meet the various and terrible needs of broken humanity. It also means that we who are Christians should be in contact in the course of the week, at work, at play, and in our neighbourhood, with people who are not Christians. It is usually more pleasurable and less demanding to spend time with Christian friends, but Jesus, our example, turned his back on all his privileges to be our Saviour, and we are called to think and act like him (Phil. 2:3-8). Even at church, do we spend our time with friends or do we seek out the needy to help them on their way to Jesus?

Tradition not God

Read also Matthew 6:1-6,16-18

We have here an example of hardness of heart different from and more dangerous than that of the confused, slow-to-learn disciples. This is the hardness of deliberate and calculated rejection of Jesus and his ministry. Consider the contrast between the people who gathered around Jesus with their needs, in the hope of help, and the Pharisees and scribes who were an official deputation from Jerusalem seeking to discredit Jesus. The 'washing' spoken of was not the normal, natural business of hygiene but the ceremonial routine of religious observance, an outward ritual that had become far more important than spiritual truth, and more important than God himself. The Pharisees ignored the teaching and the mighty works of Jesus, which had brought such blessing to so many. Of course, these men were speaking as if they were the defenders of God, his law and his worship. But Jesus challenged them by quoting from Isaiah 29:13, telling them that their religion had become more a man-made tradition than obedience to God. He went further by saying that their traditions had in fact replaced the truth of God. When this happens, the practice of religion becomes a routine, more concerned with appearances than reality, more concerned with the approval of people than with pleasing God. Some people can listen to the most wonderful, Spirit-inspired biblical preaching and find no blessing, but actually be shocked because the preacher did not wear ministerial robes. Read and ponder Matthew 6:1-6,16-18. Hypocrisy is a dangerous thing!

Hypocrisy

Read also Matthew 23:1-7,13-15,23-28

Hypocrisy is acting a part, giving the impression that things are being done for God when in fact they are done for self and for human recognition. Jesus challenged what seems to have been a common practice among the Pharisees and he referred to the commandment, 'Honour your father and mother' (Exod. 20:12), and the penalty spoken of in Exodus 21:17. This, according to the Pharisees, was the standard expected. But did they keep it? In fact, they used the religious phrase 'Corban', which meant that they had dedicated all their worldly goods to God and therefore they could not use such 'holy' money to provide for parents in need and in old age. Of course, they did not actually give all their possessions to the temple, but having 'dedicated' them they claimed that they could not give them away. They were simply acting the part of 'fully dedicated' spiritual men. They were hypocrites, and their hypocrisy ran right through the whole of their religious lives (v. 13). The Pharisees cancelled out the Word of God, substituting an iron rule of requirements and presenting God as an unfeeling taskmaster. It is said that in this religion of man-made rules the Pharisees insisted on 365 prohibitions and 248 directions. We may be shocked, but must recognize that similar rules are still with us, even in the evangelical church. Some churches try to make people conform to a 'pattern' of behaviour, or make certain 'experiences' the final touchstone of spirituality. This is so different from the real Jesus, whose yoke is easy (Matt. 11:28-30) and who came to set people free (John 8:31-36). In the early church Christians were urged to stand fast in their liberty in Christ and refuse to be brought into bondage (Gal. 5:1). Read Matthew 23:1-7,13-15,23-28. Be true, and be sure you live unto God, not unto people.

Clean or unclean hearts

Read also Isaiah 1:12-20

Jesus asks, 'Is your religion a matter of outward form and observance, or does it come from the heart?' In our professed dealings with God, do we just say and do all the right things, conforming to what is expected, assuming that by doing so we are right with God and pleasing to him? This makes religion an external thing, salvation a mechanical thing, and our walk with God a hollow performance. God looks on the heart, not just on the outward appearance (1 Sam. 16:6-7). There is of course a right kind of conformity and a sense of decency in dress and behaviour in relation to the things of God, especially when we gather for worship. But Jesus is quite clear that the 'outward' is not ultimately important. It is the heart that matters:

> A heart in every thought renewed,
> And full of love divine,
> Perfect and right and pure and good,
> A copy, Lord, of Thine!
>
> (Charles Wesley)

What is in the heart will, without question, be expressed in the life. This means that our speech, dress, behaviour, attitudes and our way of dealing with other people are all in some way indications of our spiritual life and health. When we read the list of ugly things in verses 21-22 we begin to see fallen human nature in all its potential for evil. This helps us to see the need to be 'born again' (John 3:3-7), to be given a new heart (Ezek. 36:26-27), and to face up to the challenge that we should make no concessions and give no opportunities to the 'flesh', to allow it to manifest its wrongs in our lives (Rom. 13:13-14).

A humble heart

Read also 1 Peter 5:5-10

Mark portrays Jesus on the move, possibly seeking to find seclusion and time to teach his disciples. But in spite of Jesus' desire to be private, his presence could not be hidden. Of course, Jesus is the light of the world and we who believe and follow him are also light, and it should not be possible for us to remain unknown (John 8:12; Matt. 5:14-16). We could think of verse 24 in terms of the living presence of Jesus drawing to himself those in need, or we could think of the work of the Holy Spirit, making people aware of the arrival of the one person who could meet their need. In the work of the gospel, we tend to forget about the sovereign, free and creative work of the Holy Spirit. The woman who came to Jesus was a Gentile living in Canaanite territory, and we would not normally expect faith in such a place. She may have heard the story of Elijah and the miracle his God worked for another Phoenician widow (1 Kings 17:8-24; Luke 4:24-30). She seemed to have had no doubts about Jesus' ability to answer her prayer and approached him humbly. Jesus' response seems almost brutal, even following the Jewish custom of referring to the Gentiles as 'dogs'. He stressed that she was not *entitled* to blessing, because the gospel was 'for the Jew *first...*' (Rom.1: 16). But the gospel is also for the Gentiles and Jesus was in fact speaking to her in a way that would draw out her faith. Her reply was one of total humility. She was coming empty-handed, with no claim at all, and would gladly even take crumbs from the Master's table. She may well have noticed that Jesus used the word for pet dogs, not the word for wild, mongrel dogs. She persisted in her plea, submitted herself without question, and then went home, her prayer answered.

The deaf healed

Read also Mark 5:1-20

Trace on a map Jesus' journey from Tyre, north to Sidon, then south-east in a wide detour, possibly for safety reasons, to the area of the Decapolis (the ten cities) on the eastern side of the Sea of Galilee. Think of the physical demands of Jesus' ministry! The area where they brought the deaf man to Jesus may possibly have been that of the Gerasenes or Gadarenes, where a witness to Christ and the gospel remained, as the story in Mark 5:1-20 makes plain. The conversion of that one wild delinquent could have led to a widespread Christian witness with the result that this needy soul was brought to Jesus (v. 32). There is simply no limit to what God can do with the witness of a life given over to his service. The Bible uses the illustration of yeast which, though not obvious, is effective by just being there (Matt. 13:33; 1 Cor. 5:6; Gal. 5:9). Neither, of course, is there a limit to the damage a little leaven of gossip, criticism, bitterness or moral wrong can do in a congregation and a community. The power of Jesus to transform human life and experience was manifested and the people were astonished. On a previous occasion, the people of Gadara had pleaded with Jesus to leave their community. This time they were thrilled and amazed. Consider how Jesus dealt with this needy man who, no doubt, felt his disabilities keenly. Jesus took him aside privately to assure him he was valued as a person and not just as a case for treatment. That is an important lesson for all, when dealing with other people!

Unwise enthusiasm

Read also Psalm 103:1-5,8-14

The man was taken away for a private conversation so that he could concentrate on Jesus without distraction. Jesus' actions were 'sign language', symbolic actions for a specific situation, and not a pattern to be followed by all enthusiasts for healing. As Jesus looked up to heaven, no doubt the man's eyes followed. He would sense that Jesus was saying either, 'I am from heaven and have come to you', or 'The answer to your need is from God in heaven.' The man, perhaps not yet hearing, would grasp from the lift of Jesus' shoulders that he sighed, and would know he was in the presence of 'the sympathizing Jesus'. He may even have sensed that Jesus was sharing in the burden of people like himself. We may think of the sigh as an anticipation on the part of Jesus of the death that he must yet die to break the power of sin and death in human experience. We are not sure exactly at what point the man began to hear and to speak, nor are we told what he said, nor whether he spoke to Jesus or to his family and friends. What we do know is that there was so much excitement about the blessing Jesus brought that they all forgot about the command not to tell others about it. In their excitement about a miracle they gossiped the news everywhere, no doubt attracting the attention of the authorities at a time when Jesus wanted quiet. The commotion aroused would spread the news of Jesus' whereabouts to Herod and stir his enmity. It would also tell the Pharisees where to find Jesus to continue their criticism and opposition. Unwise enthusiasm can give an opening to the devil. Be careful!

We forget so soon

Read also Deuteronomy 8:1-6,11-17

This story is very similar to the one in 6:30-44, but in 8:19-20 and in Matthew 16:9-10 Jesus is recorded as referring to two different occasions when there was a miraculous feeding of a great crowd. We are told here that the people had gathered from far and wide and for three days they had been taught by Jesus. They may well have heard of the earlier feeding of the crowd and that may have been part of the reason for their gathering. Of course, it may have been spiritual hunger that led them to gather. We just do not know, but we must recognize that people may still have a whole variety of reasons for coming to church at any given time. Some may not be clear why they have come and some may have simply followed the crowd (although there are not many crowds of this size clamouring for Jesus in our day). No matter what mixed motives the people may have had for coming, they seem to have been gripped by Jesus' teaching, and clearly Jesus gave first priority to the business of ministry. It was only after three days that the compassion he had had all the time turned to their physical needs. Once again we are told of the disciples' lack of faith, seeing only impossibilities. They seem to have forgotten the earlier miracle, failing to grasp that what Jesus had done once he could do again. This is an important lesson and we need to store up our remembrance of past mercies, past deliverances and past provision, in order to encourage our faith and to enable us to look to Jesus and to wait on Jesus whenever we find ourselves faced with a situation that humanly speaking is impossible. It is fascinating to note that at the end Jesus and the disciples were left with more food than they had at the beginning.

The clamour for signs

Read also Luke 16:19-31

Jesus went on resolutely with his ministry (v. 10). We should learn from the sense of urgency in his ministry, and at the same time note that there was no sign of panic or strain. His was an ordered life, even in the face of bitter opposition. The Pharisees, who dogged his footsteps and found endless grounds for argument and criticism, appeared once again. They asked for a sign, a miracle, some demonstration of power that would, according to them, be a compelling proof of his divine authority. But a sign is something seen, and there is no need for faith when you can see. But without faith it is impossible to please God (Heb. 11:6). The desire for signs and confirmations does in fact become an addiction. We can become dependent on them rather than on Jesus, and that leads to weakening of faith rather than its strengthening. Of course, the words 'to test him' make plain that the motivation of the Pharisees was not genuine. Jesus' reaction to the request for a sign was to sigh deeply in his spirit, and the Pharisees, who were never very sensitive to real spirituality, may not have noticed. Jesus' deep sigh (very different from that in 7:34) may indicate that once again he was aware of Satan's temptation, as at the beginning of his ministry (Matt. 4:5-7). The devil never gives up, and he nags away at the same things, the same areas of danger. In Mark's account Jesus' refusal was point blank, and he moved away from them directly and deliberately. There are times when it is not right or wise to discuss, let alone to argue. Perhaps the Pharisees thought they had won the argument, or had at least embarrassed Jesus. They may have reported back to their leaders that Jesus had been unable to satisfy their legitimate request. We do well to read Luke 16:19-31, especially the last verse.

Disciples rebuked

Read also Hebrews 5:12 - 6:3

Jesus had many disappointments in his ministry, especially among his closest disciples. He was not surprised by the dogged unbelief of the Pharisees, although he must have been grieved by it. It seems from the bluntness of his words here that he was deeply disappointed by the dullness of spirit of the disciples. As they listened in to the argument with the Pharisees, they should have been learning deep lessons about spiritual warfare and about the person and power of Jesus. But their thoughts seemed to be totally materialistic. Of course it was an indication of their sheer lack of thought that they had forgotten the practical business of organizing food. Some people are so 'spiritual' (or think they are) that the basic practicalities of life are shamefully neglected. Jesus was warning the disciples, who were destined to carry the gospel forward after the cross and resurrection, about the yeast or leaven, the dangerous spirit and attitude, of the Pharisees and of Herod. The leaven of the Pharisees was hypocrisy (Luke 12:1), a claim to and an appearance of religion that was all outward and had no real heart. The dangerous leaven of Herod was that of carnal self-indulgence and pursuit of popularity. The leaven of the Herodian party was possibly that of a spirit of nationalism that attempted to make the gospel of God into a political message. These are ever-present dangers to be guarded against, because if the devil cannot quench and stop the eager messengers of the gospel he will certainly try to distract, confuse and sidetrack them so that the truth of the gospel gets lost and forgotten. But we must note in our passage the dangerous possibility that those involved in the work of Jesus can, by careless unbelief, become hardened in heart.

Blurred vision

Read also 2 Kings 6:8-17

This chapter would have flowed smoothly if the narrative had gone on from verse 21 to verse 27, continuing the teaching and training of the disciples. And yet this incident with the blind man was a significant lesson for the disciples. As the miracle developed (a miracle does not need to be in one swift movement), the disciples were meant to see how much like the blind man they were. Their eyes had been opened and yet they were not properly focused. They were not seeing Jesus as he really was and their understanding was limited. But, with the blind man, they realized that what Jesus began he would complete (Phil. 1:6). This should be a great encouragement and comfort to us when, as often happens, we have to admit that we just cannot 'see' how Jesus is working in our, and others', lives. There is another important lesson in the story. We saw in 7:31-37 how considerate Jesus was in taking that man aside, away from prying eyes. But Jesus' action here is significant in a different way. Here he took the man out of Bethsaida and told him not even to enter the village again. This was not simply to prevent a repeat of the needless publicity that continued to hinder Jesus in his work. This village was not a place for a believer. Granted, some people brought him to Jesus for healing, but even they may not have wanted Jesus except to solve their problems. In Matthew 11:20-22 when Jesus said, 'Woe to you Bethsaida', he was really declaring that the place had no hope of salvation. Even the blind man's witness was to be withdrawn. How awful if, because of unbelief, a congregation, a parish, a city or a nation is left without a gospel witness! It happens. Some areas of Scotland that were once citadels of gospel truth and work are now the hardest places in the country.

Who is Jesus?

Read also John 1:1-4,14; Hebrews 1:1-3

Matthew 16:13-16 and Luke 9:18-22 also record this incident and add some further details. If we look back to verse
17 and remind ourselves of the confused thinking of the
disciples, we begin to see that Jesus had decided it was
now time for them to get things clear and to formulate and
express their faith in words. We do not know if Jesus' question came 'out of the blue' or if it arose in the context of
discussion. Obviously the disciples were not always exclu-
sively in the company of Jesus and they would have been
aware of all the gossip about their Master and his ministry.
Opinions were varied. Jesus was being likened to John the
Baptist, not in his stern appearance and ministry (for Jesus
was full of grace and truth), but in being manifestly a man
sent from God. Some thought of Jesus as the promised Elijah
(Mal. 4:5), whose coming would signify the great day of
God. Some thought of Jesus simply as one among many
prophets whom God sent to his people down the ages of
history. Matthew records that some thought of Jesus as being like Jeremiah, the weeping prophet, who spoke so much
in grim days about the wonder of God's love for his people
(Jer. 8:22 - 9:1; 31:3). The disciples did not mention that
some people said Jesus was in league with the devil (John
7:20; 8:48), and others that he was the son of Joseph and
Mary and no more than that (Matt. 13:55). To this day opinions about Jesus are many and varied. Some say he was
just a man; some think of him as half man and half God,
which means he is really neither; some deny he ever ex-
isted. We need to be clear that Jesus is who he is, no matter
what people say about him. We also need to be clear about
our response to him. Pilate's question in Matthew 27:22
puts us all on the spot.

The truth about Jesus

Read also Colossians 1:15-20

Jesus is the Christ, the Son of the living God (Matt. 16:16).
Peter took his stand over against all limited and false ideas
about the identity of Jesus, and so must we. He is the eternal Son of God, who was with the Father in the beginning,
the one by whom the world was called into being and
through whom the whole order of creation coheres (John
1:1-3; Col. 1:15-20). He is the very image and exact likeness
of God, and he is God's full and final word to mankind
(Heb. 1:1-3). He is the promised Messiah, the Saviour sent
into the world in the fulness of time (Gal. 4:4; John 3:16).
He is the way, the truth and the life. No one comes to God
except through him, and there is no other name given among
men whereby we must be saved (John 14:6; Acts 4:12). We
sing of the true identity of Jesus in the wonderful words of
the Christmas carols. 'He came down to earth from heaven,
who is God and Lord of all.' 'Who is He in yonder stall? ...
'Tis the Lord, the King of glory.' This is the Jesus to whom
God has given the name that is above every name, and to
whom every knee must bow (Phil. 2:9-11). This Jesus is, as
Mark affirmed at the beginning of his account (1:1), none
other than the Son of God: 'The Lord Jesus Christ, who,
being the eternal Son of God, became man, and so was, and
continues to be, God and man in two distinct natures, and
one person, for ever' (*Shorter Catechism*). Ponder well his
nature and his person. The reason behind verse 30 seems
to be that the disciples, just like the blind man in verses
22-26, were not yet seeing clearly. It is dangerous to preach
when you are neither clear nor sure about your message.

Peter does the devil's work

Read also Romans 3:19-26

Here is the proof that the disciples, especially Peter who had such potential for leadership, were still not ready to preach. Jesus was teaching his men clearly that there was a divine necessity for the Son of Man to suffer, be rejected, be crucified and rise again on the third day. God's kingdom could not come until sin and death were dealt with, and the only way that could happen was for the spotless Lamb of God to yield his life and shed his blood as *the* appointed atonement for sin. This is what Jesus was sent into the world to do. He was born in order to die, and to die as the representative of and substitute for sinners (Rom. 3:19-26; 1 Peter 1:3,18-20; 1 John 4:9-10; Heb. 9:11-14,23-28; 10:11-14). Ponder well the hymn, 'Man of Sorrows', especially the words, 'In my place condemned He stood' and think of how his enemies cried at the cross, 'He saved others, himself he cannot save.' Now consider the reaction and the words of Peter. We are told 'Peter took him', possibly grabbing Jesus roughly to contradict him. Peter rebelled at the thought of the cross of suffering and shame. Did he want the victory but not the cost? Was it love for Jesus or fear for himself that made Peter speak so radically? Did Peter think he knew more about God's plan of salvation than Jesus did? Was this not a fierce attack by Satan against Jesus at a critical point in his whole life and ministry? Jesus certainly told Peter he was doing Satan's work, not God's work, and that must have shaken the overconfident disciple. Note carefully that Jesus spoke when he saw the effect of Peter's words on the other disciples. Extravagant spiritual talk, when your own closeness to God is not what you think it is, is dangerous. You can do the devil's work and be a hindrance to God.

Self-denial

Read also Philippians 2:5-8; Luke 12:13-21

We are told in Philippians 2:5-8 that Jesus yielded his rights, humbled himself, became a servant and was obedient unto death, even death on a cross. That, said Jesus, is the way of discipleship and service. If we are to go with Jesus in this world then we must go Jesus' way. We are to give up 'self', self-will and self-pleasure, and not just give up our sins. There is no virtue in giving up our sins. We have no right to have them! We are to get out of the driving seat and give over the command and direction of our lives to Jesus as Lord. We are to have him as our example, and we must take up the cross and share in the experience of Jesus in the world, prepared and willing to suffer scorn, rejection and suffering, doing so for the joy set before us, the joy of doing God's will. In verse 35 we have a wonderful principle of life, spoken of more fully in Matthew 7:13-14. But how can life narrow down and at the same time grow ever broader and deeper? Jesus has the words of eternal life (John 6:66-68) and, as we go with him, we find ourselves sharing in the outworking and the blessings of God's plan of salvation. Jesus' words are all to do with having an authentic scale of values. There is so much that people barter their lives for, only to discover that the 'benefits' dwindle and lose value in the very process of getting them (Matt. 6:19-21). Think of the man who spent all his energies on building barns, never got the chance to enjoy them, and lost his soul in the process (Luke 12:13-21). The last word of today's passage concerns our witness, confessing Jesus by word and by way of life. This poor disordered world of ours desperately needs to hear about him and to see his grace in our lives. 'Lord, give me a chance today to speak a word for Jesus.'

A difficult verse

Read also Matthew 24:37-44

If we are honest, we must at times admit that we do not really understand what some verses refer to. The previous chapter ended with reference to the Son of Man coming in the glory of his Father with the holy angels. This seems to refer to our Lord's personal return in glory at the culmination of history. At every Communion Service we are reminded that all we do is 'until he come'. This was a constant element in the life and hope of the early church, and some thought the Second Coming would happen very soon. The truth is that it *will* happen 'very soon', unexpectedly, just when everything seems astonishingly normal (Matt. 24:37-44). That is why we are to live ready for his coming (1 John 2:28). But again and again Mark has recorded Jesus' commands to keep quiet about his power so as not to precipitate a crisis. In 8:31-33 Jesus had been telling his disciples the necessity for his death and resurrection, and they had not grasped this truth. Perhaps they grasped more readily the thought of the triumph and glory mentioned at the end of 8:38. We are all more eager to grasp at success than to face the reality of suffering. Jesus' words in 9:1 follow straight on and we are left with the statement about God's kingdom coming in power. What did the disciples make of that statement? Only some of those present were going to see this, but at the Second Coming every eye will see him (Rev. 1:7). Jesus' words, 'will not taste death', seem to indicate an event some distance away, and some people suggest that it refers to the resurrection as the beginning of the new kingdom and its ultimate victory (1 Cor. 15:24-28). But if we think of Jesus and his group of disciples, the words 'Some of you here' seem to point to what follows: the three disciples being taken up the Mount of Transfiguration.

The Transfiguration

Read also Isaiah 6:1-5; Revelation 1:10-18

Why Jesus took only three disciples and why Peter was taken after his arrogant protest and rebuke in 8:32-33 we cannot say. We tend to think of Peter, James and John as being greatly privileged, but it may be that Jesus was seeking to correct their wrong thinking. These men had leadership qualities, but if their lack of understanding had not been corrected then they would have been a danger to the work. These men did not ask for this experience. They misunderstood it and when they tried to prolong it, it was taken away, as if to emphasize that it was temporary, instructive and corrective rather than a confirmation of their spiritual superiority. What happened was that the curtain of human limitation was drawn back for a brief time so that they could see Jesus as he really was. He was transfigured, not by light shining down on him from heaven, but by the outshining of his perfect humanity. They also saw Elijah and Moses, representing the prophetic ministry and the Law of the Old Testament. These men, who had departed the earthly scene so long ago (Elijah caught up to heaven and Moses buried in an unknown place: 2 Kings 2:9-12; Deut. 34:5-6), were talking with Jesus. We are told in Luke 9:30-31 that they were talking of the departure (the exodus is the literal word) Jesus was to accomplish. The three disciples were being shown the unity and continuity of the work of salvation down the ages of history. What Jesus was to undergo in his death and resurrection was not just foretold but also prepared for in the Old Testament. All the symbolic sacrifices for sin, ordained and accepted by God throughout the Old Testament, were to be validated by the death of the true Lamb of God. This is why Jesus had said, 'The Son of Man *must* suffer.' It all depended on him.

In the presence of God

Read also 2 Chronicles 7:1-3

The three disciples were disturbed and frightened by their experience (v. 6) and at that point a cloud overshadowed the whole scene, and they heard the voice of God. The disciples, being well-taught Jews, would know plenty about *the* cloud, whether the cloud of fire that accompanied Israel in their journeys (Exod. 13:21-22; 40:34-38) or the cloud of glory that Isaiah and Solomon saw (Isa. 6:1-4; 2 Chron. 7:1-3). They would experience the same cloud later, at the time when Jesus ascended into heaven (Acts 1:9). We should think of a cloud of brightness, rather than a thundercloud. Peter, James and John would remember later that they had been in the very presence of God, that God had spoken to them, and that they had been selected to have this wonderful experience. But the final lesson from God was in verse 8: there was no one except Jesus. We must never have a fixation on our own experiences, however wonderful they may have been, especially since any special experiences may have been a concession to our weakness and lack of understanding or a rebuke to our unbelief. Think how Paul had a wonderful experience that he never spoke about for fourteen years (2 Cor. 12:1-10), and which was related to a costly burden he had to bear in order to keep him useful in service. It is so easy to become self-centred. We need to be told again and again that Jesus is everything. Apart from him we can do nothing (John 15:5). The pattern of our life and service must always be that of looking away to Jesus, looking away from self and circumstances, and seeing, as the disciples saw on the Mount of Transfiguration, that we are drawn into the ongoing, glorious purposes of God (Heb. 12:1-2).

More questions

Read also John 11:23-24; Matthew 22:31-33; Acts 23:6-8

If the Transfiguration was the outshining of Jesus' perfect humanity then, as a man, he could have claimed entrance to heaven there and then on the basis of his human sinlessness. But for the second time (Bethlehem was the first), the Son of God turned his back on the glory that was his by right and came down to be the Saviour of sinners. Jesus told the disciples not to speak about what they had seen until after he had risen from the dead and they were puzzled about what he meant. Many orthodox Jews believed in the fact of resurrection and we imagine the disciples did so too (John 11:23-24; Matt. 22:31-33; Acts 23:6-8). Jesus does not seem to have explained further, possibly because the disciples were not yet ready to be taught (John 16:12). But the disciples had their own expectations about what should happen, and they regarded these expectations as being well grounded in Scripture. They asked Jesus about the promise in Malachi 4:5-6. They had already told him that some people thought he was the 'Elijah' promised, but that does not seem to have been in their thoughts here. In Matthew 17:9-13 we are told that the disciples understood that the Elijah promise had been fulfilled in John the Baptist, whose ministry had been one of preparing for the coming of Messiah. The people had not recognized John and had dealt cruelly with him. Jesus would be treated in the same way and be rejected and killed. He insisted that the Scriptures predicted the death of the Messiah, the Servant of God. He may have been thinking of Isaiah 53, which we should read often. Perhaps the lesson is that we should read and ponder the Scriptures, and, when understanding is limited, we should wait until light begins to dawn. The Scriptures will never lead us astray.

Down in the valley

Read also Matthew 17:14-16; Luke 9:37-40

In the story of the Transfiguration we have seen the glory of the person of Christ; now we see, in the dark valley of human need, a public argument between the disciples and their critics, and the powerlessness of the disciples in the face of the boy's terrible need. We are not told what the argument with the scribes was about but it may have been that the critics were making full use of the disciples' inability to help the boy, in order to discredit the ministry of Jesus. To this day, the shallow inconsistent lives of professing Christians give unbelievers great opportunity to dismiss the claims of the gospel. When Jesus, along with Peter, James and John, arrived on the scene, Mark records that Jesus alone was the focus of attention (v. 15). The people were amazed to see Jesus. Was there something about him that drew them instinctively? It was not any shining glory, for that had faded on the mountain (v. 8). It is not clear whether Jesus' question in verse 16 was addressed to the disciples or to the scribes, but it was the father of the boy who answered. Matthew 17:14-15 tells of the father kneeling before Jesus and Luke 9:38 reveals that the boy was the man's only son. The father made clear that his intention had been to bring his son to Jesus, and only when Jesus was not there had he looked to the disciples, assuming that Jesus' men would have Jesus' power. The disciples had in fact tried to cast out the evil spirit and had not been able to do so. But they *had* been given power and had used it on past occasions, as Mark 6:7,13 makes plain. Had they assumed that this power, given for specific service, was now theirs to use as and when the occasion arose? But power belongs to God alone (Ps. 62:11, AV; Rev. 19:1) and is in his stewardship alone.

I believe, help my unbelief!

Read also Hebrews 3:12-14; 11:5-10

Jesus rebuked their unbelief and said, 'Bring the boy to me.'
This is what we must do with any and every problem and
need. Even if people will not come to church, read their
Bibles, or listen to our gentle and appealing testimony to
the gospel, we can bring them right into the presence of
Jesus. Remember the story in Mark 2:1-5 and note that the
friends did not even ask anything. They just laid the man
down in Jesus' presence and left it up to him. In today's
passage, the initial result of bringing the boy before Jesus
was that his condition got worse (v. 20), and after Jesus'
word of command in verse 25 it seemed to be disastrous
(v. 26), until Jesus quietly took the boy by the hand and
helped him up. There is no suggestion of Jesus being hur-
ried or under pressure in this whole scene. There was no
working up of emotional tension and Jesus did not wish to
draw attention to the evil spirit or to himself. His caring
concern was for the boy and his father. The gentle enquiry
in verse 21 was genuine interest but may also have hinted
to the father that he might have sought Jesus' help sooner.
The father's words 'if you can' indicate tentative faith and
Jesus at once challenged him to believe. The man knew
Jesus was not demanding perfect faith and, when he cried
out, it was a spontaneous plea not that his unbelief might
be excused but that it might be helped. We must not set
limits on what Jesus can do. We must learn to trust, because he can be trusted, no matter what the situation may
be. The man's heart-cry was answered. Think of his reaction when Jesus said to the evil spirit, 'Come out of him
and never enter him again.' Note too that the deeply personal encounter with Jesus took place aside from the crowd.
He respects our privacy because he understands feelings.

Powerlessness and prayer

Read also Genesis 18:20-33; 19:29; Judges 16:4,15-20

Have we learned the lesson taught here concerning the fundamental nature of prayer in all Christian service? The disciples were deeply exercised about the lack of effectiveness in their service, especially, no doubt, because earlier on, real power had attended their ministry (6:7,12-13). They were confused. They knew that they were chosen and privileged, but they were very slow to learn and to respond in a spiritual way. Compared to others, they were neither ignorant nor novices in the matter of discipleship. They had been used by God in the past. But that did not mean they would always be used nor that they would always be fit for use. Think of the story of Samson, whose self-confidence and self-indulgence cancelled out his usefulness (Judges 16:4,18-20). The disciples were perturbed by their lack of power. It seemed to have leaked away. There can be many explanations for spiritual listlessness and ineffectiveness. Think of the quality energy we use for so many things during the week, which can mean that we come to Sunday too tired for God. What suffers first when we are tired out? Prayer! So long as we have a sense of self-competence, or we place our confidence in methods, organization, novelty, experiments and attractions, we will not make prayer a priority. When individual and church life become crowded, and not necessarily with bad things, the first responsibility to be neglected is prayer, and the church prayer meeting. If fasting is added to Jesus' words here (as in some versions), it speaks of self-denial and self-discipline in the interest of prayer. We must not even trust in preaching alone. Prayer and preaching go together (Acts 6:4; Eph. 6:18-19; Col. 4:2-4; 2 Thess. 3:1). These two, in that order, were the marks of apostolic ministry.

The patient teacher

Read also Isaiah 52:13 - 53:12

The disciples thought they were ready for spiritual service and even when they were subjected to the discipline of failure (9:14-29) it seemed to make little or no difference. The amazing thing is that Jesus did not despair of them, nor did he consider rejecting them and starting with a new group. He went on and they went on with him (v. 30). Again there was a determined policy by Jesus to keep the disciples and himself out of the public eye and away from the clamour of confrontation, argument and public enthusiasm. His great burden was to prepare his men for the future, in which they would have to play a significant part. The thing they had to grasp was that the heart and the dynamic of all the work of God's kingdom were to be the death and resurrection of Jesus Christ the Son of God. The disciples knew the Scriptures that spoke of the Son of Man (Dan. 7:9-14), and no doubt at least three of the disciples could link that with what they had seen of Jesus on the Mount of Transfiguration. They also knew the Scriptures that spoke of God's Suffering Servant in Isaiah 52:13 - 53:12. What they could not grasp was that the glorious person, whose origin was from before time, was the Jesus born in Bethlehem (Micah 5:2), who must die for the sins of his people. They could not understand that their Jesus was the one promised by God and sent forth by God to be the atoning sacrifice for sin (Rom. 3:21-26; 1 John 4:9). Again and again Jesus made it perfectly clear that the cross was to be no accident. This was God's plan, and in due time Peter would see it, rejoice in it and preach it with conviction by the Holy Spirit (Acts 2:22-24). But here, the disciples did not understand. Why they were afraid to ask will be evident in the next verses.

Pride exposed

Read also 1 Corinthians 3:1-7; Ephesians 3:7-8

The disciples were not always side by side with Jesus and that must have meant there were many occasions when our Lord would have borne the burden of his ministry and his approaching death quite alone, without any human compassion or support from those to whom he had ministered such blessing. When Jesus saw them talking so earnestly among themselves, did he long that one of them might come and talk to him? No one did. In the house at Capernaum Jesus asked them what they had been talking about. This does not mean that he was grieved at being left out because he knew full well what the topic of conversation had been. He knows his disciples and what they talk about. None of them answered Jesus' question. At least they did not say, 'Nothing in particular', because that would have been a lie. Which disciple started the discussion about importance and precedence we do not know: Peter, James and John may each have felt that the experience at the Mount of Transfiguration and at Jairus' house indicated their importance. Peter may have protested that he was the spokesman on the Mount and at Caesarea Philippi. Andrew may have pointed out that he was the one who brought the boy to Jesus for the feeding of the crowd. Judas may have pointed out coldly that he was the trusted treasurer and administrator of the disciple company. Others may have felt aggrieved that they had not been singled out for any particular privilege. Why is it that so often we want recognition for 'all we do' for Jesus? Is it not a privilege to be fellow-workers with him? Is it not true that apart from him we can do nothing (John 15:1-5; 1 Cor. 3:5-7)?

Childlike not childish

Read also Philippians 2:1-11

It would have been so easy for Jesus to administer a stern rebuke to the disciples because their pride was hindering them from learning and from becoming the kind of men God wanted them to be. Instead, Jesus spoke kindly but searchingly, recognizing that mixed up with their pride there was in fact a desire to be God's true servants. He told them that the only way to be 'something' in God's service was through a willingness to be 'nothing'. Of course a desire to be something is not the same as wanting to be somebody. The first is a desire to be useful to God and the second is a desire for recognition. Jesus called a child to stand in the middle of the group. He had no sentimental illusions about children. He knew that children can be self-centred, manipulative and ruthless, and can demand a great deal of time, attention and energy. What was the lesson? Jesus was teaching the disciples to be childlike not childish! The child would have been surprised at suddenly being the focus of attention and yet happy to be in the arms of Jesus. In the ways of the world, a child would never be promoted to high office nor would the child expect it. It is the simplicity and unselfconsciousness of the child that Jesus was emphasizing. He had been chosen by Jesus and was with Jesus. That was his reward. Read the verses of the hymn, 'Father I know that all my life is portioned out for me,' (Anna L. Waring). Note how they speak of the restless person always seeking for some great thing to do. The hymn shows that cultivating a true fellowship with Jesus is the heart of service. The last words of a verse of that hymn sum this up: 'Content to fill a little space, if Thou be glorified.'

We are the people?

Read also Matthew 7:1-5,21-23

It is almost unbelievable that John should burst out with these words in such a situation and atmosphere. Perhaps it was because he was one of the youngest of the disciples. Perhaps it was reaction to Peter. Perhaps it was because he felt that Jesus did not appreciate his evident love for him. The disciples seemed to be falling into the all-too-common snare of thinking that they and they alone were the true servants of Christ and his kingdom. We know from Scripture that people may 'use' the name of Jesus, although they are not in any sense Jesus' servants (Matt. 7:21-23; Acts 19:13-16). In this instance Jesus did not cast doubt on either the power or the sincerity of those who had cast out demons, and so set human lives free. We must always recognize that others are used by God, often in different ways from ourselves. Sometimes both methods and motives are suspect, but whenever Christ and the gospel are preached we should be glad. That is Paul's message in Philippians 1:15-18. It does not mean that we accept everything at face value, especially where false doctrine is taught (Gal. 1:6-9; 2:11; 2 John 10). But God advances his work in a variety of ways, all of them sovereign and sure, even though mysterious to us. Sometimes a sense of insecurity or even jealousy causes us to criticize and even condemn others. Sometimes we are too quick to defend our own leaders; wise leaders are aware of this and reassure their people (Num. 11:26-29). We should always pray that many more will come to speak and preach in God's name. Jesus points out that sometimes simple acts of kindness, not arbitrary tests, show who is the Lord's and who is not. The final thing to notice is that it was powerless, ineffective disciples who were criticizing those whose activities were attended by God's blessing.

A solemn lesson

Read also John 15:1-6; 16:12-15

When the disciples forbade the man to preach they may have prevented some needy people from hearing the gospel. Now Jesus spoke solemn words of warning regarding the possibility of causing children, or young disciples who are children in the faith, to sin or to stumble. We must watch carefully how we deal with others and make sure that our attitudes, actions and words do not hinder them from fervently following Jesus. We must not undermine a child's simple trust in Jesus or in the Bible, nor must we hinder a young believer by loading him or her with our particular doctrinal rigidity or our church order preferences. The Pharisees in Jesus' day exercised a tyranny of rules and regulations that simply strangled spiritual life. We *do* seek to teach the whole counsel of God, but only as people are able to receive it (John 16:12-15). Think how slow some of us were to learn! Jesus also says we must watch how we ourselves behave. The hand, foot and eye seem to refer to the whole range of activity and involvement in our lives, and if any of these things is a hindrance to our commitment to and service of Christ, then we should get rid of it, however painful that may be. If we do not, we will live to regret it. Jesus uses strong images to encourage seriousness but does not mean literal mutilation of our bodies, as some have suggested. Solemn though it be, we must also recognize that in these words Jesus is affirming the reality of hell in the world that is to come. Of course there is a wrong and gruesome way to speak about hell, but we must not hide the fact that the spiritual issues of the gospel, faith and unbelief, being for Jesus or against Jesus, have consequences that are eternal. We have to be serious.

Salty or tasteless

Read also 1 Peter 1:3-7; 4:12-16

Jesus had spoken seriously about the fire of judgement facing those who refuse to part with their sins, which have a
sinful effect on others. But there is also a fire of purification. The 'saltiness' of our lives gives us, and the society in
which we live, a healthy flavour, and it will also act as a
preservative against corruption. This saltiness will be produced in us by the fires of trial and testing. This is spoken
of in 1 Peter 1:6-7; 4:12-14. J. B. Phillips translates James
1:2-3: 'When all kinds of trials and temptations come crowd-
ing into your life, don't resent them as intruders, but welcome them as friends. Realize they come to test your faith
and to produce in you the quality of endurance.' Jesus may
have been referring to the salt added to a sacrifice in the
ritual of Leviticus 2:13, indicating to the disciples that a
life given to God for service is not complete or worthy without this quality of 'salt'. The words 'Have salt in yourselves'
seem to mean 'Be right in yourselves.' The words, 'Be at
peace with each other' emphasize to the disciples that their
spirit of competition and criticism has no place at all in the
company of Jesus nor in his service. Jesus makes plain here,
as he did in the Sermon on the Mount (Matt. 5:13), that
even privileged disciples and men and women who have
been used greatly in the past can, in fact, lose the distinc-
tive saltiness of a heart and life that are right with God. The
sour taste that can so easily quench the healthy, salty savour
of life is usually pride: spiritual pride, that assumes its own
superiority.

The question of divorce

Read also Genesis 2:18-25

Daily notes are not the place for a full study of divorce and remarriage. Note the circumstances of today's passage. There was a crowd, and they would be fully aware that some of the Pharisees were very strict, allowing no divorce, and others were so lax that they allowed a husband to divorce his wife for almost any reason. The Pharisees' motive was to test or to trap Jesus, assuming that, whatever his answer, one section of the crowd would react badly, and so call into question Jesus' whole ministry. The Pharisees thought they were on a sound basis when they quoted from Moses (Deut. 24:1-4), who seemed to allow divorce for 'something indecent', which they interpreted as anything the husband did not like. They did not quote Genesis 2:24 and we should always be suspicious when people are selective in their quotations from Scripture. Jesus' words in verses 6-9 confirm that God's pattern and principle at the beginning still holds. In Genesis 2:18, we see that marriage was not instituted as a restriction on human fulfilment and happiness, but so that man and woman together in this special relationship might be able to attain to and fulfil the glorious destiny and service of their humanity. It was God who 'invented' marriage and it is always wise to go by the Maker's instructions. It is a fact of life that there are problems and hurts in marriage relationships, but in considering them we must start on the highest ground, with what God ordained, not with human rights and desires. Jesus recognizes that all sorts of influences make us what we are, and marriage, or singleness, or failed marriage are not the factors that mark us out as fulfilled, dedicated, spiritual or unspiritual. The secret of life and service lies in the glad acceptance of what our good and gracious God ordains for us.

Marriage breakdown

Read also Matthew 5:31-32; 19:1-12

We must read carefully and think clearly. Jesus pointed out that it was because of the hardness of men's hearts, which includes disregard of the hurts of women and the effects on children, that Moses 'concession' was instituted. It was not meant to make divorce easy but rather to make people think, to realize that the break was irreversible, and to give the woman some legal standing by having an official certificate that would need to specify the actual grounds of divorce. Note the strong legal and moral position given to the divorced wife in verse 11, and the equally strong caution given to the woman in verse 12. However difficult it may be to come to a clear position regarding the issues raised, Jesus gives no support at all to the notion of easy divorce and equally easy remarriage. We must, of course, give due weight to the 'exceptions' spoken of in Matthew 5:31-32; 19:9 in relation to marriage infidelity, and also in 1 Corinthians 7:15 where the unbelieving partner leaves the marriage due to their rejection of the other's Christian faith. These serious cases are seen to break the marriage and the wronged partner is free to remarry. Nothing is said here about physical brutality or mental breakdown and cruelty. People say, 'Marriage is not the bit of legal paper but love.' Is it then just a human decision, the legal act and the consummation? No. Marriage is God's ordinance, part of God's order for creation, given to some and withheld from others in God's secret but perfect wisdom. Society can be strong, healthy and happy only when the marriage bond is held in highest honour. But we must be careful not to make marriage failure the only area of human experience where there is neither forgiveness nor a new beginning. A new beginning is a gift of God's grace, not an automatic human right.

The children

Read also Galatians 3:6-7; Psalm 103:13-18

When parents argue about their 'rights' to freedom from unsatisfactory marriage and to remarry, their children tend to be forgotten. It may have been Jesus' words about marriage that caused people to bring their children (Luke 18:15 says they were babies) to Jesus. It was not unusual for parents to bring children to one of the rabbis to be blessed. The fact that Jesus took these children in his arms and blessed them does not mean that anyone who wants a baby baptized should have their request granted without question. We must not build a doctrine of baptism on these verses. The children, and perhaps even the parents, would have little understanding of what was going on but this did not cause Jesus to reject them. When the disciples held them back, Jesus was indignant, insisting the children should come to him. In what sense are we to understand that the kingdom of God belongs to children? It cannot mean that 'naturally' they belong to the kingdom (Eph. 2:3; Ps. 51:5). Jesus says that he, the King of the kingdom, belongs to the children as much as he does to the adults. It has nothing to do with deserving or with childlike innocence, but all to do with the Saviour coming to them. We are not dealing here with a 'baptism' or a 'blessing' that automatically makes children part of God's kingdom for ever, regardless of their future response and obedience. Presumably the parents, having brought their children to Jesus, would continue to teach them 'by prayer, precept and example' so that, having grown up in an atmosphere of faith and obedience, they would in due time become obedient to God. If God's blessings and privileges are rejected in disobedience they are forfeited. Not all who are marked by the sign of God's covenant prove to be God's people (Gal. 3:6-7; Rom. 9:6-8; John 8:37-40).

The rich young ruler

Read also Luke 18:9-14

The life and blessing of the kingdom of God have to be
received as a total gift, not earned or deserved. That was
not the attitude of the rich young ruler. He did not think of
himself as helpless or empty-handed, even though he realized that he was not perfect. He came to Jesus, just as the
parents had done with their children, but he had quite a lot
to say for himself and he felt quite sure Jesus would be glad
to have someone like him as a disciple. He was rich, young,
a ruler of the synagogue (Luke 18:18), highly regarded in
all circles, and the disciples may have been thrilled at the
possibility of such a 'catch' to add to their company. Why
do we tend to think the conversion of some important person
is more significant than that of others? But in spite of all he
had and had achieved, he knew that the real desire of his
heart had not been fulfilled. He asked about eternal life. It
is interesting that Luke 18:9-14 records the parable of those
who trusted in themselves and it seems the ruler had no
thought of *his* need to be put right with God. His running
to Jesus indicates earnestness, but his words in verse 20
suggest he regarded his religion and his good living as his
strong points. Jesus pointed out that the title 'good' belonged
to God alone, giving him the opportunity to confess, as Peter
had done earlier, that Jesus was none other than the promised Christ sent from God. Jesus loved this young man, and
longed to draw him into the kingdom of God.

The sad ruler

Read also Matthew 6:19-24

Jesus spoke only of the manward side of the Ten Commandments (Exod. 20:1-17), but it is not clear just what 'defraud'
refers to, unless it means coveting. Did the rich man covet
even more? Possessions and success can lead to greed and
the condition becomes addictive! The young man's answer
in verse 20 was quick, guileless, and without any sense of
need. If there was anything else for him to do he would do
it, or so he seems to have said. Jesus told him the one thing
that stood in the way of eternal life: his riches and all the
comfort, social standing and self-congratulation they gave
him. These were the things that really mattered in his life.
His riches and what they signified were the centre of his
interest. In a moment the young man may have become
aware of the earlier commandment that required people to
have no other 'gods' taking priority over God. Jesus challenged him, not in spiritual and theological terms, but in
practical surrender of life. The man's face fell. He was not
being welcomed with open arms. He was not being given a
graduation certificate. He was being called to the obedience and surrender of discipleship. He did not think of
himself as a sinner, let alone a helpless needy one. He did
not seem to be aware of the love Jesus had for him. He went
away in sorrow, and that may be a good sign, especially if it
led to a reassessment of his life's attitudes and priorities.
His life was just so full, there was no room left for God.
That is something we all need to think about. The man
went away, and Jesus let him go.

The danger of riches

Read also 1 Timothy 6:6-10

The disciples seem to have been shocked by the incident, perhaps thinking Jesus had been far too hard on the young man who seemed so eager in spiritual longing. The disciples needed counselling about the danger of riches. Riches of various kinds, personality, intellect, talents and popularity as well as cash, can make people lose their sense of need in relation to God. Jesus does not say it is wrong to have riches, because if God has blessed us in this way we have immense opportunities to do good, to serve and to support God's people and their work in the world. But if we trust in riches (as the footnote to v. 24 indicates), we are in danger, because our trust will not be in God. God is permanent but riches are fickle and temporary. It is the *love* of money that leads to all kinds of evil and can lead people away from faith. Read 1 Timothy 6:6-10. Ponder it carefully and test your own thinking about life. If you surround yourself with things and people so that they take first place in your life, you may be erecting barriers that will keep you from ever becoming a real part of God's kingdom. The disciples were shocked by Jesus' words, reacting rather cynically (v. 26). If there was no hope for a promising and hopeful person like the ruler, what chance was there of anyone being saved? At least they were thinking about salvation. Such concern is amazingly absent from the thinking of worldly and 'religious' people alike these days. We need to be saved. There is sin, judgement and hell to be saved from, and if we remembered this, our praying and preaching would both be more earnest and urgent.

The reward of discipleship

Read also Romans 5:1-5; 2 Corinthians 4:16-18

Salvation *is* impossible if it is thought of essentially as human effort (Rom. 3:19-20). Salvation is the work of God's sovereign, saving grace, by Jesus Christ, in the power of the Holy Spirit, through the preaching of the gospel. Immediately following Jesus' words in verse 27, Peter began to speak. He was always too ready to speak, too ready to affirm his own spirituality, but he was not allowed to finish. Jesus interrupted him to make a statement that should quench all spiritual pride. Jesus did not deny the cost of discipleship nor did he belittle what it had cost his disciples to leave all and to follow him. But he did insist that there are compensations and rewards in this life and in the life to come. No matter how costly it has been to follow Christ, no matter how many failures, no matter how often we have had to be rebuked by Jesus for our slowness and pride, would any of us go back to a life without him? Think of Paul's words in Romans 7:16-21, and of the fearful apprehension of Mary Magdalene as she thought of former evils laying hold on her life again (Luke 8:2; John 20:11-18). Jesus honestly confirms there will be persecutions. But these will not spoil, or reduce the blessings (Rom. 5:1-5; 2 Cor. 4:16-18; James 1:2-3; 1 Peter 1:3-9; 4:12-14). Paul speaks of the fellowship of Christ's sufferings as a privilege and blessing greatly to be desired (Phil. 3:8-10). The sacrifices involved in true discipleship vary from person to person, because the Lord deals with us all in perfect wisdom and balance. What he takes from one, he may allow to another. How he deals with one person or family may differ greatly from another. We must not make comparisons. Instead of wondering who is first and who last, we should marvel that we have been given a place at all.

Heading for the cross

Read also John 12:20-33

This is a vivid picture of Jesus in the lead, striding on with great purpose, heading for Jerusalem. There is no need to pity Jesus, for he was not in any sense a victim of circumstances. He was going to Jerusalem to do the very thing for which he had come into the world (John 12:27). We can only try to imagine the burden of his heart (Luke 12:49-50), which came to full human awareness in Gethsemane (Luke 22:39-46). Some of the crowd following Jesus were afraid, possibly aware of the risk in going to Jerusalem. The disciples were amazed, full of foreboding when they should have been aware of the positive nature of the impending crisis. It is easy to criticize confused and struggling disciples and to see the shallowness of their understanding and their spirituality, but they were still followers. Even Thomas, who seems to have had a depressive personality, went on with Jesus (John 11:8,16). We must see in the fear of the disciples, and in their slowness to understand, the work of Satan. His enmity was against the disciples who were marked out for future service, but also against Jesus who had to go forward without the fellowship, understanding and human support of his closest friends. Of course, the disciples were still a group rather than a fellowship. When Jesus saw their hesitation, he took the time to teach them again, in specific detail, what lay ahead of him in terms of his death and resurrection. As he spoke to them he must have been aware that they did not really understand. Their minds and hearts were clouded and confused and their thoughts were so centred on themselves that, as early as this, Jesus stood alone. This is part of the cost of that 'dying to self' that leads to fruitful service. C. H. Spurgeon said, 'There is no loneliness like that of a soul that has outstripped its fellows.'

Desire for place

Read also 1 Corinthians 4:1-7

James and John, perhaps urged on by their ambitious mother (Matt. 20:20-22), show a terrible insensitivity towards Jesus who had just spoken of his suffering and death. The two brothers deliberately excluded Peter, of whom they may have been jealous and resentful because he was always pushing himself forward as the spokesman for them all. They seem to have assumed they had a special relationship with Jesus that qualified them for honourable positions. Did James and John think of themselves as superior because their father had a business and employed servants? Some Christians feel that if they have wealth or intellectual qualifications they are necessarily spiritual. Peter, James and John had been given special privileges but it would not have occurred to them that their 'extra' experiences might have been given because Jesus saw that they were more in need of help than the others. There was no doubt an element of faith in the brothers' request, because they spoke of Jesus' glory as certain to come. Perhaps the saddest thing, even more disturbing than their pride but closely linked with it, was the fact that they seemed to have no sense at all of their spiritual limitations. They did not hesitate in their assured reply in verse 39. It is wonderful that Jesus did not rebuff them. He caused them to consider whether or not they were able to share his sufferings or whether they were seeking to go beyond their spiritual capacity. Read Romans 12:3, a wise and necessary caution.

The pattern for service

Read also 1 Corinthians 3:1-15

This passage is searching but encouraging. Little as James and John knew what they were saying and committing themselves to, Jesus accepted them. They would share, more than they knew, in the sufferings of Jesus that led to glory; and that is privilege, as they would soon discover (Acts 5:40-42). Jesus must have impressed the disciples with his answer in verse 40, making it plain that even he did not look for or ask for place, privilege and recognition. As Philippians 2:5-8 makes plain, the royal Son of God forfeited all his rights and privileges and became a servant. That is the pattern for all service. At the end of the day places are given to those who prove themselves worthy to occupy them in the world to come. Ponder passages such as 1 Corinthians 3:1-15; 4:1-5. What are we doing with our lives and the opportunities for service that come and go so quickly? Are we building for eternity in a superficial way that will leave us with regrets? Are we building for the future so that those who come after us will have something worthwhile to inherit? Remember Jesus' story in Matthew 7:24-27 of the two men who built their houses in the same area. The house without a real foundation did not even last a lifetime. Think of James and John, so eager for recognition and prominence. In due time James was martyred for the faith (Acts 12:1-3), and died aware that Peter was in prison awaiting execution. John, in his old age, was exiled to Patmos (Rev. 1:9). They did indeed drink the cup Jesus spoke of.

The devil gets in

Read also 1 Peter 2:18-25

See how Jesus dealt with the heated resentment of the disciples. The ten were indignant. Who did these brothers think they were, setting themselves up as 'top-class'? This was a satanic attack on the unity and peace of Jesus' company and must have been a sore distraction for the Master at such a significant stage in his ministry. The disciples may have been focusing on Jesus' words recorded in Matthew 19:28, which suggested that all twelve of them would have thrones. Jesus was stern and clear with his chosen men, because if this attitude of pride became established their future service would be distorted before it even began. All who would serve Christ must learn deeply that greatness has nothing to do with place and prominence but everything to do with willing and humble service. Some who have both place and recognition have no real spiritual power in their lives and service, simply because they lack this servant attitude in which 'self' dies and is willing to be nothing so that Christ can be everything. Think of the story in John 13:1-16 when none of the disciples was willing to do the humble task. Jesus is always our example. It does not come naturally to be like him (1 Peter 2:18-25). It is painful to be reviled and scorned, and only a deep work of God's grace in our hearts can enable us to react as Jesus did. Read verse 45, and think well and often about Jesus who paid the ransom price (1 Peter 1:18-20) to buy us back from sin's dominion and set us free to live. The cross Jesus spoke of to his disciples was indeed dark, grim and costly, but it was to be glorious not tragic. In the light and shadow of that cross there is no place for pride.

A blind man sees

Read also Matthew 20:29-34; Luke 18:35-43

Matthew and Luke also record this story but there are a number of differences. Were there two blind men? Was the incident (it was more than a mere incident to Bartimaeus) as Jesus entered Jericho or as he left the town? Why do Matthew and Mark tell of the blind beggar but say nothing of the other miracle in Jericho, the opening of the eyes, heart and life of Zacchaeus (Luke 19:1-10)? Reporters nowadays never give identical stories but this does not throw doubt on the facts. Jesus' passing through Jericho was a significant time because he was on his way to Jerusalem to die and would never pass that way again. For many, and we are told only of Bartimaeus and Zacchaeus, it was a once-in-a-lifetime opportunity. Bartimaeus may well have had some sense of this urgency, some awareness that this was his only chance to go to Jesus of Nazareth, who had done so much for others, and that made him shout out. The details are so vivid that Mark must have been told the story by an eyewitness, no doubt Peter. Mark names the man and his father, tells us of the change in attitude of the crowd when Jesus showed interest, and describes the excited reaction of the blind man when he realized Jesus had stopped (vv. 46,49-50). Despite the crowd, Jesus immediately attended to one needy individual who cried out to him. Jesus did not rebuke the man for identifying him as 'Son of David', even though at other times he insisted that the disciples, and others, should keep quiet about his identity and the purpose of his coming death (cf. 8:30). How much faith he had and to what extent Bartimaeus was aware of who Jesus was we cannot tell. But he had no doubt as to what he wanted Jesus to do, nor of Jesus' ability to do it (v. 51). We do not have to wait until our faith is perfect before we come to Jesus.

Still in Jericho

Read also Luke 19:1-10

The life of Jesus was full of incident, crowded with sudden meetings that changed people's lives. Two notable miracles took place in Jericho where Jesus took a personal interest in two very different people, who were both in great need. The blind man was a beggar, possibly with no home or at best a hovel (although rich, professional beggars were not unknown); and Zacchaeus, the prominent citizen, was one of the wealthy class. Both men were spiritually deprived and they both, in different ways, acknowledged this. One man climbed a tree, forgetting his dignity, while the other man shouted and made such a fuss that everyone rebuked him for distracting them. No one seemed to criticize wealthy Zacchaeus, but many were quick to put the unimportant beggar in his place. When Jesus stopped, what a lesson it was for the crowd who had at first so devalued Bartimaeus! They had an immediate change of heart, offering reassuring words (v. 49). Imagine the eager anticipation of the crowd as well as Bartimaeus. There is simply no experience better than seeing before our eyes the awakening and the confirming of faith in someone we know, especially someone whose conversion we may have prayed for and yet felt it would never come. Jesus' question in verse 51 did not suggest ignorance of the man's need. It was to give Bartimaeus the opportunity to put his faith into words. That is always important (Rom. 10:8-11). There is so much to learn from Jesus about personal work in the gospel. Mark does not tell us of the changes in Bartimaeus' life after his meeting with Jesus, but Luke tells vividly of the change in Zacchaeus' whole attitude to himself, to others and to his professional life.

The King comes

Read also Zechariah 9:9; Psalm 24:7-10

Everything Jesus now did was done deliberately. When he rode into Jerusalem on the colt, he knew that the pilgrims gathered in the city in preparation for the Feast of the Passover would see his action in terms of Zechariah 9:9. The Passover celebrated God's great deliverance of his people from the tyranny of Egypt. It was deliverance for a spiritual purpose, but in Jesus' day the dominant desire was for a political deliverance from the power of Rome, because the political masters of the Jews were cruel as well as powerful. But at the same time the power of Rome guarded the peace, upheld a measure of justice, and facilitated travel in a way that was to prove vital in the early days of the spread of the gospel after the resurrection. We must never assess political and sociological situations without reference to spiritual issues and to the sovereign providence of God, to whom alone power belongs (Ps. 62:11, AV; Dan. 4:17; Rom. 13:1-5; 1 Tim. 2:1-2). Jesus would have been fully aware of the explosive state of people's feelings when he made this public presentation of himself as the long-expected King and Saviour. But he was never directed or diverted by public opinion, especially when that opinion was more driven by tradition and human expectation than by spiritual knowledge instructed by and grounded in God's Word. Over against the 'coronation' enthusiasm of the Jewish crowd, think of the derision (tinged with anxiety) of the Roman authorities at this spectacle of a lowly king. People see different things, depending on whether they look with faith, unbelief or scepticism.

The Prince of Peace

Read also Luke 19:37-44

The arrangement about the colt may or may not have been made in advance by Jesus. He and his ministry were well known and many, as well as the close disciple band, had responded in faith. As soon as the colt's owner knew it was Jesus who wanted it, he was willing to give it. We who have received so much from the Saviour should all react in the same way. We should be ready and willing to give what we have: our time, our energy, our talents and, indeed, our cars (the equivalent of the donkey) to be used by him. But note the gracious, human consideration of Jesus in the promise that the animal would be sent back as soon as possible. Perhaps it was a necessity for the owner's livelihood. Notice particularly that no one had ever sat on this animal and yet there was no wild or fearful reaction or resistance on its part, even in the midst of the shouting, waving crowd. This was not the result of training but simply the awareness of the animal that the Lord of Creation sat on its back. Those who have watched horses with their handlers will know how important the hands and the voice of the rider are. Think then of Jesus calming the colt. Think of the calm poise and regal demeanour of Jesus in the midst of the crowd and think of him as the Prince of Peace. He knew why he had come to them and what he must do for them. He was not taken in by the enthusiasm of their shouts nor was he deterred by the kind of criticism recorded in Luke 19:39-40.

Jesus in the temple

Read also Matthew 21:1-13; Luke 19:28-44

Matthew and Luke record more excitement and emotion than Mark does. The entry to Jerusalem was significant but are we right to speak of it as the triumphal entry? In a sense it was; the King was presenting himself to his people, and he was worthy of all admiration. We do not err when we sing on Palm Sunday,

> Ride on, ride on in majesty!
> In lowly pomp ride on to die;
> Bow Thy meek head to mortal pain,
> Then take, O God, Thy power, and reign.
> (Henry H. Milman)

Luke records that Jesus wept over the city. Matthew suggests Jesus went right to the temple and exercised his authority as the Lord of the temple. But Mark makes plain (no doubt told by Peter who would have been there watching) that it was a very quiet Jesus who went to the temple, walked around its courts, taking note of everything, and then departed to spend the night in the peace and detachment of the home of his friends in Bethany. There were many important things to do but Jesus did not act impetuously. What an example this is to us, especially when we see so many things that seem to be a contradiction of and a hindrance to the life and work of God's house. There is no suggestion that, even though it was late, Jesus was too weary to go on. He may have been aware that his close disciples had gone through enough for one day. No one objected to the idea of going home. Did they talk? Did they pray? Or did they follow the Master's example and sleep to be ready for a new day? To rest is sometimes the most spiritual thing we can do.

A visual aid

Read also Luke 13:6-9

Many are puzzled as to why Jesus should speak such a word of judgement against the tree because it lacked fruit when it was not the season for figs. We cannot possibly think that it was just a reaction by a hungry Jesus, angry because there was no fruit. That would be a contradiction of his whole personality. Only the close disciples were with Jesus and therefore the 'message' of the incident was for their instruction and benefit. The area of Bethphage (the name means 'house of figs') was covered with fig trees which, we are told, produce their first figs before the leaves appear. From a distance Jesus saw one tree already covered with leaves, ahead of all the rest, and thus claiming priority and superiority. Jesus was entitled to expect fruit but there was none, and the tree was exposed as being a fraud, claiming much but providing nothing. The tree was a 'hypocrite'. But the fig tree was recognized by the Jews as a symbol of Israel, and that is the point of Jesus' parable in Luke 13:6-9. Much care and attention had been lavished on Israel as God's chosen people, and they were proud in their claim to be that special people. They were God's people in name but where was the fruit that confirmed their calling? We have to understand this seemingly strange incident as a parable, or a visual aid, the meaning of which the disciples would soon see. Israel had been given so many blessings and privileges (Rom. 9:4-5; Isa. 5:1-7); God had been so patient and forbearing; but their day of grace had run out. Their privileges were being withdrawn, as Jesus said so clearly in Matthew 21:33-45. When a people profess much but produce nothing, their life is a fraud. Read Revelation 2:4-5; 3:1-3.

Cleansing the temple

Read also Jeremiah 7:1-11

This was not something done in a surge of anger but a considered action on the part of Jesus. He entered the temple as God's appointed Priest and did what the other priests should have done long before. God's house should be a house of prayer (Isa. 56:7; Jer. 7:11) and those who defiled it by introducing things which, at their best, were worldly and, at their worst, corrupt and defiling, would be rebuked by God. The ritual of the temple was being observed with accuracy but the administrators were using God's house and the cloak of religion to make money by corrupt means. The pilgrims who came to offer sacrifices could buy the appropriate animals in the temple courts. If they brought their own animals, the priests could pronounce them unclean, and they had no option but to buy: at a price! The temple tax had to be paid in Jewish shekels and foreign money could be exchanged: at a price! The priests may not have done the actual selling and exchanging. That might have soiled their spiritual reputation, so they rented out stalls in the Court of the Gentiles (not regarded as a spiritual part of the temple), the rent going to themselves and, no doubt, Caiaphas, the high priest. The Court of the Gentiles was also where the 'outsiders' seeking after God were confined to. What impression would they get of God and his holiness from such a clutter of godless bargaining? What impression do people get when they enter *our* churches? Do they become aware of God and of people seeking him? When they hear about all the activities taking place, are they made aware of eternal things? What would Jesus say about our churches? Are they really places of worship where people expect to meet God and hear him speaking to them? What is our attitude when we go to church?

Love for God's house

Read also 2 Chronicles 7:1-3,11-16

Mark records this incident as taking place at the end of Jesus' three years of ministry, when the final move towards the cross was already set in motion, and the build up of resentment and enmity on the part of the Jewish religious leaders had reached murderous intensity (v. 18). John 2:13-22 records this incident near the start of Jesus' ministry, and comments that Jesus was motivated by zeal for God. Of course, our zeal has to be controlled and directed by love, grace and wisdom. We must be right in ourselves and right with God before we can begin to cleanse God's house of activities and attitudes that serve only to hide both God and the gospel from those who are in need. Some people find it easy to criticize what they feel is wrong in the life of the church, but Jesus' heart must have been deeply grieved as he took this stern action. Remember that the whole day was not occupied entirely by the cleansing of the temple. It was a day of teaching, because symbolic action divorced from teaching can lead to confusion. People need to be taught why certain things are done in God's name. That is why, at the start of a ministry, where there has been no real biblical teaching, a minister must be particularly wise and patient. That evening, as was his usual custom, Jesus returned to Bethany. No doubt he spent time in prayer alone, but he also rested and was refreshed by fellowship with his trusted friends, Mary, Martha and Lazarus. At this stage the disciples were far from understanding or sympathizing (see Matt. 26:6-13). Although Jesus was mighty in spirit he was also totally human. Think how much more difficult it would have been for him if that home and family had not been there to minister to him. Spiritual service takes many forms, practical caring as well as praying.

Have faith in God

Read also Luke 7:1-10

Morning saw Jesus and his men again on their way to Jerusalem and as they passed by the withered fig tree Peter remembered the words of the previous day. We cannot tell to
what extent Peter had understood the meaning of the curs-
ing of the fig tree but it seems he was surprised that it had
happened so quickly. Jesus could well have said, 'What did
you expect?' but instead he spoke words which could be
understood as challenge or command, 'Have faith in God.'
The call to faith is set over against the surprise Peter showed.
Jesus seems to emphasize the need to fix our eyes upon
God who speaks, acts and deals decisively, and swiftly when
necessary, with all things and people in relation to his work
and his kingdom. This is the God who speaks and it is done
(Gen. 1:3). There is neither uncertainty nor limitation, and
even when his ways are mysterious and past finding out
(Rom. 11:33), they are wise, wonderful and accurate. Jesus
went on to deal with two matters issuing from faith, namely
prayer and forgiveness. Jesus cannot be referring to literal
mountains being removed, because that would lead to all
sorts of grotesque ideas. He was using a common Jewish
phrase that referred to the removing of difficulties. His challenge to his disciples, when faced with huge problems, was
to take them to God in prayer, at once and not as a last
resort. With God, nothing shall be impossible (Luke 1:37).
But for us, to be 'with God' means to be gladly and serenely
surrendered to his will and to be walking in obedience with
him. The authority that moves mountains and makes the
way plain for God's work to be done is an authority that
belongs to and rests in God alone. It was this authority the
centurion saw in Jesus (Luke 7:1-10) and his faith was
commended and received its answer.

Believing prayer

Read also Matthew 26:36-44

In verse 24 we have a staggering statement about prayer. But it has caused some people to indulge in what may be called 'autosuggestion', trying to *make* ourselves believe that what we pray for *must* happen. This is a wrong attitude to prayer, turning our eyes away from God. It forgets that at times, for his perfect purposes, God denies even the most earnest prayer of the most godly people. Paul's sore cry to be relieved of some terrible affliction was not granted (2 Cor. 12:7-9). Yes, we must pray in faith not in doubt, but when our focus is on *our* praying and the answer *we* want rather than on God, his perfect will and his perfect power, we become confused and fall into error. People can become burdened and even crippled with guilt, feeling, 'If I had prayed more', or 'If I had had more faith or been more earnest', someone might have succeeded or someone might not have died. Undergirding all our praying is God's good and perfect will, and our prayers must be in harmony with his will, even when we do not know or are not clear as to what that is. Think of Jesus in Gethsemane: 'If it is possible … but as you will' (Matt. 26:36-39). It gives us great relief and assurance to know that if we are asking wrongly God will not grant it. But there are also times when, because of our perverse and stubborn wilfulness, God grants our request but sends leanness to our souls (Ps. 106:13-15, AV). If God, by his Spirit, puts it into our hearts to pray in faith for some specific answer then we must persist in it, not doubting, even if the answer is long in coming. God works to appointed times (Hab. 2:3) and he does give this kind of burden (2 Sam. 7:25-29; 1 Chron. 17:25,27). We also have the wonderful encouragement in Isaiah 65:24. Jesus said, 'Have faith in God.'

A right spirit in prayer

Read also Matthew 18:21-35

The NIV places verse 26 as a footnote but other versions include it in the main text. Jesus is teaching his disciples and us that our attitude to others is basic in our praying. He is not speaking here of forgiveness of sins in relation to salvation. That forgiveness is once-for-all on the basis of the atoning death of our Saviour Jesus Christ. The issue here is our attitude to and our dealings with others. If we hold an unforgiving spirit against those who have wronged us, refusing to forgive when we ourselves have been forgiven so much by God, something is very wrong. Our profession of faith can be challenged. Read Matthew 5:21-24, where there is no actual mention of *us* having a grudge against a brother. The brother may have an exaggerated idea of our wrongdoing. All the more reason to go to him. Matthew 18:21-35 is so vivid and searching that it needs no comment. We should remember how utterly miserable we have felt when wronged, neglected and taken for granted by those we have ministered to, cared for and supported. It can be so easy to pay them back in their own coin, to stand aloof, and say 'Once bitten, twice shy'. But if that is our attitude, can we really go and pour out our prayers to God, expecting him to care, hear and answer? Jesus taught us to love our enemies, but can we have enemies within God's redeemed family? God generously forgives us. Think of his mercy, peace and love added together, then multiplied and poured out on us who deserve none of it (Rom. 5:5; Jude 2). Our Lord Jesus Christ is our great example who, when he was reviled, did not answer back (1 Peter 2:21-25). He was willing to be the humble servant (John 13:1-5,12-17). An unforgiving spirit makes us bitter, so that we cannot speak openly with God on our own behalf, let alone in prayer for others (Ps. 66:18).

Answered by a question

Read also 1 Peter 3:13-17

Jesus made his way to the temple where representatives of the three main groups of the leaders of the Jewish people came to challenge him about his actions, particularly the cleansing of the temple, which they regarded as a totally unwarranted intrusion into the area of their authority. Their question was 'What right have you to take leadership and authority in the things of God?' These men knew all about Jesus' ministry and mighty works. They knew also that his ministry carried with it an authority from God that they did not have (Mark 1:22). But their reaction was one of total rejection in spite of all the evidence (John 7:32,45-52). Jesus refused to answer their question until they answered one of his and he presented them with a challenge (vv. 29-30). They had a private discussion among themselves, recognizing they had been outwitted, and replied rather pathetically that they could not answer. There must have been many in the crowd who heard Jesus' final word with great pleasure, seeing these proud men obviously embarrassed and defeated. Now we must note carefully from verse 33 how Jesus proceeded. He did not enter into further discussion, nor did he in any sense seek to explain his authority or defend his teaching and his actions. Even if he had, these men of fraudulent spirituality would not have been persuaded. No matter what Jesus said or did, they had already made up their minds that they did not want him. There is a lesson here in personal witness and evangelism. At times we must refuse to be drawn into argument, even when we feel we have a totally valid answer. Remember how Jesus stood silent before Herod, who wanted an interesting discussion about religion and God (Luke 23:6-9). We must learn to be both wise and gentle (Matt. 10:16).

Faithless servants

Read also Isaiah 5:1-7

The leaders and the crowd would almost certainly recognize this parable as being based on Isaiah 5:1-7. In Matthew's Gospel three parables are recorded together: the son who said yes, but did not go to do his father's will; this parable, which Luke also records; and the parable of those who refused the king's invitation to the marriage feast (Matt. 21:28 - 22:14). In one brief parable here Jesus summarized the whole story of the Jewish people down the ages of history. Their existence as a people, their protection, prosperity and privileges as the servants of the kingdom were all the gift of God. They had been put in charge of what belonged to God so that his vineyard would bring forth fruit. In God's goodness, they would be allowed to share this fruit. But with amazing persistence, when God sent his messengers the prophets to look for the fruit of obedience, the people rejected and persecuted them. The leaders of the Jews had taken the work that belonged to God and regarded it as their own, resenting what they saw as God's interference. Be quite clear, God's prophets were not sent to take away from the people their blessings and privileges, but to lead them on in the service of God, which was the way of life. But as God spoke and called, they resisted his words. They would not listen. They had to be told in plainest terms. Stephen declared the same truth in Acts 7:30-60 and it cost him his life. Jesus said these things here and it cost him his life. This is a solemn reading, but the same hardening of heart and the exposure of unbelief are still seen in our day in many churches all over the land. How we should pray for the preaching of God's Word, that the Holy Spirit will work in sovereign gracious power, so that the Word will be received in faith (John 16:7-11; Heb. 4:1-2)!

Dangerous unbelief

Read also John 1:1-3,9-13; 3:16-19

Jesus was making plain that the rejection of God's Son was
no accident. It was deliberate unbelief. God had made one
final appeal, had spoken one final word that declared his
love, and had sent his own Son (Rom. 5:6-8). Link verse 6
of today's passage with the devastating comment in John
1:11. Verses 7-8 stress the enormity of the sin of rejecting
Jesus. It was totally deliberate, with recognition of who and
what the Son was. Before the end of the week the men now
hearing Jesus' parable would be confirming the evil of their
hearts, which Jesus was exposing, by shouting with venom,
'Take him away! We have no king but Caesar!' (John
19:12-16). They were prepared to deny their history, their
identity, their religion and their destiny in order to get rid
of Jesus. We are told two things in verse 9. There is an ines-
capable judgement involved in deliberately rejecting Jesus.
That is clear from John 3:16-19. The judge is God himself.
The people being judged and set aside were God's chosen
people whom he had blessed and privileged in so many
ways for so long. But the work they represented, which
they had carried forward down the ages, is God's work,
and that work is not allowed to fall because of the sins and
failures of God's people. The kingdom would be taken from
them and given to others who would prove faithful and
fruitful (Matt. 21:41-43). The priests would be challenged
by the quotation from Psalm 118:22-23 over the possibility
that the 'stone' they were rejecting was, in fact, the head
cornerstone of God's spiritual temple. Using familiar
Scripture, Jesus was still seeking to awaken them to a true
awareness of God and to call them to repentance and faith.
But it was all to no avail, as verse 12 makes plain. Their
rejection was clear and they went away.

A clever question

Read also Romans 13:1-7

Unbelief will try anything and use anyone in order to continue opposition to Jesus and his work. The Pharisees prided
themselves on their spirituality and the Herodians majored
on their nationalism. They had little in common except
their opposition to Jesus, which had gone on from the start
of his ministry (3:6). The Pharisees tended to be rigid in all
their attitudes and the Herodians tended to be 'political'
and to compromise. The question, designed to trap Jesus
into making a public statement, was disguised as an issue
relating to faith and spirituality: how to obey and please
God. The crowd was interested because, like today, people
were not keen on taxation. If Jesus said, 'Pay your taxes', he
would have been out of favour with the people. If he said,
'Do not pay your taxes', his enemies would have instantly
reported him to the Roman authorities as a troublemaker.
Jesus, calm and assured and knowing their hypocrisy, asked
for a coin. They produced a Roman coin, which every male
had to use to pay the Roman tax. Jesus asked his question
and pointed out that they were using Caesar's coin, thus
accepting that they were living under a regime that had
brought them peace, roads and a measure of justice. If they
accepted the benefits then they must also accept the responsibilities. They should pay back to Caesar what belonged to the state by right. Think about this. Our generation concentrates on rights and privileges, with little gratitude for what it has materially and spiritually, and often
with little enthusiasm for paying for its own or others' benefits. But, as Christians, it is our duty to render to Caesar
what is his by right. We must also give back to God what is
his by right. He has total claim over us. We are not our own
in any sense, we are bought with a price (1 Cor. 6:19-20).

What about heaven?

Read also 1 Corinthians 15:12-20,35-43

The persistence of evil unbelief in its various forms is staggering. In spite of the pointed message of the parable (vv. 1-12) and the equally devastating defeat of the scheming questioners (vv. 13-17), the rationalist Sadducees came with a religious conundrum in an attempt to mock and discredit Jesus. They quoted Scripture (Deut. 25:5-10), the arrangement whereby the name of a family would be preserved through the generations. The Sadducees, who did not believe in any resurrection at all (Acts 23:6-8), asked this question either to make Jesus look ridiculous or to show that this provision given by God made it impossible to believe in a resurrection of the dead. They thought they were being clever at someone else's expense, as unbelievers still try to be. These men must have been taken aback when Jesus said so pointedly that they were wrong in their thinking and therefore in their conclusions. Those who refuse to believe in resurrection are always wrong (1 Cor. 15:12-20). It is wrong to think of heaven and the life of heaven in the restricted terms and concepts of the life we know on earth. The Bible says the life of heaven is better than this life (Phil. 1:23); it is a fulfilment rather than a reduction (2 Cor. 5:1-5); it is described in glorious negative terms, the absence of all the things that spoil our enjoyment of this life (Rev. 21:3-4). The life to come corresponds to this life in the way the fully ripe corn corresponds to the seed sown, and it is God who gives the resurrection body as the appropriate and effective way by which the redeemed personality can express itself in life and service (1 Cor. 15:35-43). We must not reduce or limit the reality of the life of heaven simply because it is beyond our power at present to understand it.

More thoughts of heaven

Read also Revelation 21:1-7

The Sadducees were asking about a world they did not believe in. They were the kind of people who insist that reality can only be as great as their own human intellect. That is sheer pride, as well as foolishness. Some people today insist that if something cannot be seen, measured and reduced to a statistical formula, then it cannot be. What right have we to assume that there cannot be any form of life other than what we now know? A child cannot grasp the delights of love and marriage, nor can a newly married person enter instantly into the rich maturity of long years of true partnership. A non-Christian cannot see, let alone experience, the spiritual truths of the kingdom of God, not even if he is religious like Nicodemus (John 3:3-9; 1 Cor. 2:9). The Sadducees' did not know their own Scriptures and so did not know God. Verse 25 does not cancel out the rich blessing of Christian marriage, of two made one by God. To speak of being like angels in heaven does not mean a non-physical existence, but rather one that is free from flaw or limitation. The Sadducees thought of marriage simply in terms of the propagation of the species. Jesus took these men to the very Scriptures they claimed to believe in. God said, 'I *am* the God of Abraham, Isaac and Jacob', not, 'I *was* their God when they were alive' (Exod. 3:6). If God was a friend to Abraham during his life on earth, how much more is he now in heaven? Physical death cannot cancel out God's love and covenant. The Sadducees would not have been pleased to hear Jesus publicly proclaim, 'You are quite wrong.' Many today know little about God and are afraid to think about heaven. D. L. Moody said, 'One day you will read in the papers that D. L. Moody is dead. Don't you believe it. I will be more alive that day than I have ever been before.'

The commandment

Read also Deuteronomy 6:1-9; Leviticus 19:18

The whole passage from 11:20 - 13:37 covers one day of questions and teaching. Throughout it all we see the peaceful authority of our Lord Jesus. Wave after wave of opposition came against him. The disciples were confused and uncertain. Some people came with what seemed genuine enquiry and desire, and others were challenged and rebuked publicly. What a costly day it must have been, and there was the rest of the week to come, culminating in Good Friday. In today's verses we find one of the scribes, having listened in to the discussions with Jesus, coming with what seemed genuine spiritual concern. But the scribes were teachers of God's law and this man was no doubt fully conversant with the religion of rules laid down by the Pharisees, no less than 613 commandments, so scholars tell us. The man may well have been feeling there was more to serving God than a list of regulations and so he asked which was the most important commandment. Jesus' response was immediate and without any note of rebuke. He quoted first from Deuteronomy 6:4-5, the affirmation that orthodox Jews repeat daily, then from Leviticus 19:18, which sum up the Godward and the manward aspects of the Ten Commandments. The scribe answered Jesus with relief, not in a patronizing way, acknowledging that the heart of true religion is not in observance and ritual but in love to God, from which flows love to others. Why should we love God in this wholehearted way that sets the direction and gives the impetus to our manner of life? Because he first loved us (1 John 4:19). If our love to God is genuine, it will soon show in the way we treat people (1 John 3:16-18; 4:11,20-21). In verse 34 Jesus indicates that although the man *wanted* God he was not yet aware of how much he *needed* God.

Jesus' question

Read also Matthew 21:9-11; Luke 19:37-40

The last statement of verse 34 sets the scene for today's verses. It seems that Jesus' responses had produced a spirit of willing listening among the crowd in the temple and he took the opportunity to teach them, first about his own person and identity, and then concerning true religious practice. Jesus asked the question, 'Who is Christ?' He made the people think. Was God's promised Messiah just a man, a Jew like themselves, someone they could co-opt to the Sanhedrin or elect to be a leader, someone with whom they could sometimes agree and at other times disagree? Was he just a human descendant of David, or was he more than that? Jesus took the people and the scribes to the Old Testament. He referred to Psalm 110, emphasizing that it was inspired by God. The crowd, the scribes and the Pharisees would all remember how Jesus was hailed on Palm Sunday as the King coming in the name of the Lord (Matt. 21:9-11; Luke 19:37-40). If they recognized him as the King promised by God and now sent among them, the question they had to face was 'Who is he?' How could he be just David's son, when in the Psalm David refers to him as Lord? Jesus, of course, was fully aware of who he was. He knew the answer to the question that baffled the scribes, giving the crowd such pleasure. David's Lord was the eternal Son of God, who became David's son when he was born in David's town of Bethlehem. These verses may be difficult to grasp but Jesus was dealing with a misunderstanding that exists to this day in religious circles and society in general. Jesus is not just a good, kind man who teaches sound moral principles. He is God's eternal Son, who came 'from highest bliss down to such a world as this' (John 1:1-3,14; Micah 5:2; Isa. 9:6-7). Of course, unbelief will never see this.

The danger of prominence

Read also Matthew 6:1-6,16-18

Having silenced the teachers by the question they could not or would not answer, and having grasped the attention of the crowd, Jesus proceeded to speak in the plainest of terms. He warned the people against listening to teachers and preachers who are manifestly unbelievers, especially if they have doubts and reservations about the divinity of the Lord Jesus Christ. Jesus charged the scribes with being primarily concerned with being recognized and praised by the people. It was their self-importance, linked of course with their desire for popularity, that was being exposed. They liked to think that they and they alone had authority in spiritual things. They were indignant if they were not given their proper place on public platforms. What a warning there is here to all who are in any way called to be in the front line in the context of the life and work of Christ's church. Who are we trying to impress? Is it human recognition or God's approval that really matters to us? Read John 12:43. Jesus' charge goes even further. He speaks of those who sound very spiritual but whose practical lives do not reflect this. Their dealings with others are not honourable. Their financial affairs are suspect. They try to cover up their various frauds by long prayers that sound very spiritual. This is hypocrisy and, because it is deliberate, God will bring such people to judgement. Read Matthew 6:1-6,16-18. None of Jesus' searching words should cause us to stop praying in a prayer meeting. Silence may be just another way of covering up the fact that we are spiritually adrift. The call is to be real in our daily lives, and in our spiritual service to be honest with God. God knows whether we are spiritually alive, or if we just have a reputation (Rev. 3:1).

Two little coins

Read also 2 Corinthians 8:1-15

This could be a disturbing story to think of the Lord Jesus Christ watching people put in their offerings. Of course he does see all we do, why we do it, and in what spirit. It is said that there were thirteen trumpet-shaped brass receptacles for donations to the various aspects of the work of the temple. It may have been that the rich, with a visible flourish, put money into all thirteen offerings. Among the rich there may well have been the rich young ruler (Mark 10:22). Without question there would have been quite a crowd of watchers interested in who gave what, and possibly impressed by those who gave large sums. The offerings would all be in coin and would make some noise as they dropped in, but the widow's two coins (Who told Jesus the amount? Did he just know?), valued at a fraction of a penny, were very thin and would drop in with scarcely a sound. With the rich around her putting in so much, she may well have felt that in comparison with others her offering was totally insignificant. For eleven of the thirteen offering boxes she had nothing. But Jesus saw her, recognized the nature and true value of her offering, commended her publicly, and dared to compare the giving of the rich people unfavourably with hers. The rich gave substantially, as they should, whatever their motives. The clear suggestion is that they could afford it and that there was not a great element of sacrifice involved. The widow did not calculate whether to give a tithe (a tenth) from her gross or net income. She gave all she had. The two coins may have been her day's wage, and if so, there was nothing left for food. The simplicity of the story is searching. Little wonder Jesus called his disciples' attention to the woman's action. Would Peter remember his words recorded in Mark 10:28-31?

135

Christian giving

Read also 2 Corinthians 9:6-14

Money is a touchy subject but stewardship is part of Christian discipleship and service. It is a spiritual issue. In 1 Corinthians 16:1-2, immediately following glorious truth about the resurrection, Paul reminds the Christians about systematic, as opposed to impulsive, giving. In 2 Corinthians 8 and 9 Paul teaches those who were proud of their striking spiritual gifts the principles of Christian giving without actually mentioning money, comparing their giving with that of others (2 Cor. 8:1-5). They must prove their love for the Lord in their giving (2 Cor. 8:8-14), as it is a test of their faith and witness. We are to be responsible in our giving. Some may question the wisdom of the widow who gave so sacrificially to a religious system that was manifestly far from what God wanted it to be. But there was no other temple, or 'church', and even with its limitations and corruptions, it provided a recognizable place for people to gather for worship. It may also have done a great deal of good in practical terms. Even the grim story of Judas shows this (Matt. 27:3-7). But perhaps the widow had heard Jesus say that this was his Father's house, and it was to God, in response to his love and grace, that the widow gave so sacrificially, and for this she was commended by the King and Head of the Church. In the 1960s a frail, hunchbacked student, now in glory, regularly walked from the Bible Training Institute to church. One Sunday she had no money at all, but had one postage stamp left. She sold it to a fellow-student so that she would have something to put in the church collection. That kind of giving is recorded in heaven. In God's eyes, giving is measured not by amount but by proportion, sacrifice and love. Of course, time, energy and care should also be given to God, who has given us all we have.

A great building

Read also 1 Kings 19:10-18

Those who have visited modern Jerusalem, or who have seen illustrations, will have some idea of the vastness and impressive nature of the temple and its courts, which cover some 500 by 400 yards. This building was begun in 19 B.C. and was still being built forty-six years later (John 2:20). It was finally completed in A. D. 63, and destroyed by the Romans in A. D. 70. For the Jews, the temple was the symbol of the greatness and glory of their God and of his presence with them. In the time of Jesus the Jews were under the dominion of secular Rome, and the religious life of the temple was not held in true regard, although the main feast days were still observed. But the leaders of the Jews, the people, and even the disciples, felt that as long as they had the temple, things would work out. Even with the wonderful teaching of Jesus so recently ended, one of the disciples spoke admiringly of the temple as they left it. After all, Jesus had called it his Father's house. Imagine the astonishment that must have followed Jesus' words in verse 2. Even today in Scotland people say, 'We still have the national church.' But no building or religious establishment has automatic permanence. If the life of God's house drifts away from its God-given spiritual priorities, its obedience to God's Word and the fundamentals of the faith as they are focused in the person, life, death, resurrection and coming again of the Lord Jesus Christ, then collapse is inevitable. If the foundations are destroyed even the righteous can do little (Ps. 11:3); yet God never leaves himself without a witness, even in the darkest days (1 Kings 19:14,18). Long-established religious institutions may go, but there will always be a remnant of faith. Buildings may go, but God's foundation stands sure (2 Tim. 2:19).

Signs of the end?

Read also Matthew 23:37 - 24:8

The disciples seem to have accepted that Jesus was speaking about some significant, coming crisis because they asked 'When?' not 'Why?' nor 'How can this be?' They asked for information about signs or indications of when this crisis would come, so that they might be ready for it. In Matthew's account (Matt. 24:3-5) the disciples seem to have asked about three things: the destruction of the temple, the coming of Christ in his glory, and the end of the age; and they seemed to think of all three happening together. As they sat on the Mount of Olives, no doubt looking over to the impressive temple, Jesus' first word to them was to be careful lest they be deceived. He warned that false 'Christs', religious frauds, would come on the scene, with powerful personalities and an appearance of spirituality. They would prey on people's fears and gullibility, emphasizing the nearness of the end of the world, and many would be led astray. Jesus warned of coming political and international upheaval in wars and crises, together with physical calamities such as famines and earthquakes. These do not necessarily indicate that the world is coming to an end. In fact these are the ongoing travail of world history. They are the beginning of the birth pains (v. 8), that is, they are bringing into existence something new and better. These sore experiences in the world are not futile, nor are they insignificant. In his sovereign providence and purpose, God is working out his plan for the fulness of the time (Eph. 1:10). Now, the Bible makes it plain that whenever God is at work, bringing salvation, and building his church for its eternal destiny, then the enemy, human and spiritual, will be active in opposition. We must not be surprised when this comes and we ourselves are affected.

Times of trial

Read also Acts 4:1-4,13-22

Jesus explains what it will mean to some, and indeed to all in some measure, to be involved by faith in what God is doing in the world, at all times and especially in times of crisis. It will be particularly intense as the end of time draws near, for that will bring God's final victory, and 'the devil ... because he knows that his time is short' will be particularly angry, even desperate (Rev. 12:12). Jesus repeats his warning to be on guard (vv. 5,9). All disciples need to listen carefully when we are being taught because we never know when we will need that teaching in a very particular way. God may be saying to some as they read these words, 'Be very careful today.' In verse 9 Jesus speaks of bitter opposition and persecution from both religious and secular authorities. There will be a significant swing of public opinion against Christian truth, standards and way of life. There will be pressure on Christians to conform to 'accepted' ways and to keep quiet about the Christian message. But these very pressures are to provide the opportunity for witness. Read, for example, Acts 4:1-4,13-22. There will also be sore and costly division within families, and some who profess the Christian faith will be disowned and others betrayed to the authorities, who will put them to death. But Jesus gives assurance that, in spite of all, the gospel will be preached. The gates of hell will not prevail (Matt. 16:18, AV) and the gospel will reach out to the nations. We must not fear, because at the right time and in the right way, the Holy Spirit will enable us to give testimony in God-given words (v. 11). Jesus' words are a comfort in crisis, not an excuse for careless preparation when we are called to minister God's Word. We are to stand our ground; events will reveal the false and the true, and those who endure to the end will be saved.

Time to be careful

Read also Daniel 11:28-32; 12:11

These are difficult verses and we must not try to fit them into a scheme of prophecy and its interpretation. We approach the passage by asking first what this must have meant to the disciples in their day, and then what it means and how it applies to us now. If we wonder why the words of verse 14 are so vague, we must remember the tense political situation in Jesus' day. Our Lord would not speak in extreme terms that the Romans might regard as treason, and Mark, recording the incident, would also have to be careful because he was writing his Gospel when the destruction of Jerusalem was not far away. There is a lesson here for those who tend to 'speak their mind' without considering if it is wise or appropriate or necessary. Of course, the disciples, being good Jews, would link the mention of the abomination that causes desolation with Daniel 11:31 and 12:11. That was history. The Assyrians invaded Israel in 167 B. C. and sacrificed swine on the altar in the Jews' temple. Jesus is warning his disciples that the Romans would also desecrate the temple. This did take place and the people of Jerusalem were treated terribly. The scenes would be similar to what we see and read about in places that suffer 'ethnic cleansing' in our own day. Jesus said it would not be a time for bravado, but for seeking safety. When we come to verses 19-23 it seems that Jesus' words point much further forward than the destruction of Jerusalem in A. D. 70, to the events that mark the end of time. The picture is vivid and alarming. But at the same time we look at Jesus' words in Matthew 24:36-39, where the coming again of Christ in glory is described as being a time of ordinary living, but with an almost total absence of thought of God. The picture is certainly contemporary.

Read the signs

Read also 2 Thessalonians 2:1-8

When we see sacrilege and blasphemy asserting themselves brazenly and deliberately in the presence of God, we know the times are solemnly significant. As Christian believers we must be aware of how this evil attitude is affecting and manipulating the whole atmosphere and behaviour of society in our day. We cannot run away, but we can and must pray (v. 18). When we hear of a city church being ransacked, the pulpit Bible torn to shreds and the Communion cups trampled on, what are we to think? There have always been peaks and troughs of horror, atrocities, affluence and complacency, and verse 19 says things are going to get worse. These themes were part of early apostolic preaching (2 Thess. 2:1-8). The prospect would be almost unbearable but for Jesus' words in verse 20. There is control. God himself sets the limits to which evil is allowed to operate, all in the interest of his people and the work of salvation. 2 Thessalonians 2:6-8 emphasizes the spirit of lawlessness, significant in our own generation. Far from things being beyond God's control, he acts swiftly by 'the breath of his mouth'. The key to the whole of history, right to its climactic end, is God's plan of salvation. Part of that plan is to expose evil for what it is, so that its judgement is seen as both necessary and righteous. We must learn to see God at work in world history, and if we cannot see, then we must believe, because it is true. There will be false prophets speaking comforting words, saying, '"Peace, peace," when there is no peace' (Jer. 6:14; 8:11). False messengers, religious, scientific and philosophical, will speak wonderful words and show marvellous things to allege we do not need God. Take heed to what Jesus has said. That is the safest preparation for what lies ahead.

The day of the Lord

Read also 2 Peter 3:3-13

People today talk about the changes in weather patterns and we hear far more about earthquakes, floods and other convulsions in nature, but these words of Jesus seem to speak of even more radical happenings. In spite of the ending of the 'cold war' we hear about more and more nations having nuclear capacity, and the possibility of world conflagration is real. The 'end of the world' is a concept that no longer seems fanciful. Read the vivid description in 2 Peter 3:8-13 and note that the emphasis is the same as in Jesus' words here in Mark. The end is not destruction, but a completely new order of existence in which right-eousness dwells in full and perfect harmony. In that new order of things the Son of Man, the Lord Jesus Christ him-self in the full shining of his glory, will gather from the whole earth and the whole of history his own chosen, be-lieving, ransomed people. Whatever is meant in verse 25 by the heavenly bodies being shaken, it is quite clear that the emphasis in the passage is that, as history comes to its convulsive but glorious climax, there is complete and total and continuing control. It is not man, and certainly not the devil, who brings the world to its destiny of salvation and judgement. Everything, to the smallest and greatest detail, is in God's hand. All sorts of things may yet happen. Things we have not even begun to imagine may burst in on our human experience. But the truth for the believer is that our lives are hidden with Christ in God (Col. 3:3), and we are assured that there is nothing, known or yet to become known, human or demonic, natural or supernatural, that has the power to separate us from the love of God in Jesus Christ our Lord (Rom. 8:35-39).

The Second Coming

Read also 1 Thessalonians 4:13 - 5:4

Right through its history the church has believed in the personal return in glory of the Lord Jesus Christ. Every time the Apostles' Creed is repeated we say the words, 'From thence He shall come to judge the quick (or living) and the dead.' His coming again is spoken of in Acts 1:11; 1 Thessalonians 4:13-18; Revelation 22:12,20; and in many places in the four Gospels. Always the emphasis is on the fact, its unexpectedness and its immediacy. Some people say the Second Coming has been expected for a long time, and yet it has not happened. In their thinking they postpone it to some far-off time, so far off that it becomes irrelevant. It is helpful to think of the world of time and the world of eternity in terms of two parallel lines, separated by the most minute distance. The coming of the Lord is simply Jesus stepping through the veil and he is here. That is why we must be ready. There will be no time for last-minute preparations. But Jesus said that there were signs to be seen and understood. In verse 30 no doubt he was speaking to the generation of the disciples, but his counsel is also for us. Be quite clear, in the Bible, the 'last days' are the days from the birth of Jesus to his return in glory (Heb.1:2; 1 Cor. 10:11; 1 John 2:18). In today's passage, Jesus speaks about the whole order of life and existence as we know it passing away and ceasing to be. That is hard to imagine, but we have Jesus' words, and he says they stand for ever (v. 31). We must study them, believe them, be guided by them, and we must also rest in them. But first of all we must ensure that we are ready in terms of salvation. We must be in Christ, for there is salvation in no other. No one but Jesus the Saviour can bring us safe to heaven (John 14:6; Acts 4:12).

Until he come

Read also Acts 1:11; Revelation 1:7-8

Although these passages have been solemn, we must not come to the end of the chapter with a feeling of alarm and apprehension. After all, it is the Master whom we love and serve who is returning. When our eyes have really seen the glory of the coming of the Lord, we will gladly sing, 'Glory, glory, hallelujah!' Think of the hymn, 'Lo! He comes, with clouds descending, once for favoured sinners slain,' (John Cennick and Charles Wesley) and the hymn, 'Christ is coming! Let creation from her groans and travail cease' (John Ross Macduff). In every Communion Service, as we remember our Saviour's dying love and rejoice in it, we remind ourselves that it is only 'until he come'. We have never *seen* Jesus, except as we have seen, known and understood him in his Word (1 Peter 1:8). But we shall see him in person (Rev. 1:7). We will rejoice in his victory and understand a great many things that have baffled us throughout our lives. The doctrine of the Second Coming must never be used as an escape from responsible involvement in this needy world. Nor must it be used to frighten sensitive souls, especially children, with thoughts of the separation of believers and unbelievers. We must not speculate about times, and timetables of prophecy, because the timing of the great day is a secret kept by God the Father alone (Matt. 24:36). If Jesus is content to wait, so must we. But that is not the same as idleness. Read verse 34 and see the privilege and the responsibility of being trusted servants of the Master. Each has his work, allocated according to the Master's will. Watching and working are not in contradiction. We want the Master's house to be ready for him, and we want to be ready ourselves.

Plan to murder

Read also Luke 22:22; John 10:17-18; Acts 2:22-24

These verses, together with verses 10-11, set the context and atmosphere for the lovely story in verses 3-9. The passage begins with the chief priests and scribes in earnest discussion as to how to get rid of Jesus permanently, and it ends with Judas Iscariot's solution. It was drawing very near to the time for the solemn events of the sacred feast of the Passover and these 'spiritual' leaders of the Jews had to see that all was done according to the strict requirements of God's law. At the same time they were plotting the deliberate murder of a man who had done no wrong. Their desire to kill was nothing new. Early in Jesus' ministry they had resented his spiritual power and authority (Mark 3:6). Now, three years later, their slow burning enmity had been brought to flash-point by his triumphal entry to Jerusalem, his cleansing of the temple, and by his searching ministry that had challenged their position and exposed their hypocrisy. The enthusiastic 'Hosannahs' of Palm Sunday had made it clear that popular opinion ran in Jesus' favour and they knew they needed some secret way to gain their end. They said, 'Not during the Feast,' but God had ordained the timing for the sacrifice of the true Passover Lamb. The decision was not in the hands of religious hypocrites nor of the traitor Judas. Jesus' life was not going to be taken from him. He was going to give it up willingly. John's account emphasizes God's hand on every event leading to the cross (John 2:4; 7:30; 8:20; 12:23,27; 13:1; 17:1). It is deeply moving to see God's plan working out with such perfect timing, because it helps us to consider the dignity, majesty, poise and willingness of the Saviour as he proceeded so deliberately to his death. These verses should reassure us when we are faced with deliberate opposition to the work of God.

A beautiful thing

Read also John 12:1-6; Psalm 69:20

We turn from the grim bigotry of unbelief to the sweetness and light of true faith, devotion and gratitude. The picture is both beautiful and sad, the costly devotion highlighting the action of the betrayer. The company was gathered in the house of Simon the leper and, according to John 12:1-6, Jesus' friends were there. Martha, always well organized and willing, was serving. No doubt all present, perhaps even Judas, admired Jesus because he had done so much for them. But only one seemed to be aware of the burden of the Saviour's heart, and only one actually *expressed* gratitude, love and faith. Perhaps Martha agreed with what her sister did; we would like to think so. The men, as is so often the case, were slow, perhaps reluctant to express what they really felt. Matthew 26:6-9 tells us the disciples were indignant, perhaps because it was a woman who took the initiative, but officially because they had a concern for the poor. Jesus' words of rebuke to the company made it clear the men had failed: failed to discern true spiritual devotion, failed to have true spiritual priorities, and failed to come alongside their Lord when he was beginning to go through the deepest trials of his life and ministry. If ever Jesus felt alone it must have been then. Would he have thought of Psalm 142:4 or Psalm 69:20? We do not know to what extent the woman (Mary, cf. John 12:3) was aware of the nearness, the significance, and the costliness of Jesus' death, but she knew that the Son of God loved her and would die for her, and she did not hesitate in what she did. She would have agreed that, 'Love so amazing, so divine, demands my soul, my life, my all' (Isaac Watts). Was Mary's action extravagant? Jesus obviously did not think so. It certainly was not done to impress, but to express her love, gratitude and faith.

The betrayer

Read also John 13:21-31

The story of Judas is a solemn subject. We are told quite clearly that Judas was one of the Twelve, the inner company of Jesus' followers. He had been there from the beginning and was the trusted treasurer of the company, although read John 12:4-6! Some commentators have tried to whitewash Judas, suggesting he acted as he did in order to save Jesus from the consequences of his own radical ministry. This is total nonsense. Judas' going to the chief priests was not a sudden reaction to the incident with the woman's devotion. It was the inevitable culmination and exposure of what he had been from the beginning. In John 6:66-71 Judas is described as a privileged man, called into the company of Jesus. When many went back from following Jesus, Judas stayed, but even at that early stage he was already under the influence of the devil and not in sympathy with either the person or the work of Jesus. All along Judas held to his earlier profession that he was really one of the disciples. Now we are told he went to the chief priests with the deliberate intention of betraying Jesus, for which he was to be paid. He then returned to his place among the disciples in the upper room, and was there when Jesus washed the disciples' feet. Judas' feet had already trod the road to his consultation with the chief priests. The point of no return came as they all sat at table together at a time of holy fellowship, teaching and spiritual significance. Satan took final possession of the hardhearted unbeliever who had resisted every influence of grace throughout his three years with Jesus. Matthew 27:3-5 records Judas' final dark remorse, linking it with the hard indifference of the chief priests. How we must guard against an evil heart of unbelief that will always take us away from God (Heb. 3:12).

Preparing for the Passover

Read also Exodus 12:1-14

It is a relief to turn from Judas (although he was still in the company of the disciples) to the quiet, serene composure of Jesus. He, and he alone, was in command of the situation in its every detail. The disciples were sent to look for what would be most unusual: a *man* carrying a water-pot. The guidance would be unmistakable! It came to pass exactly as Jesus said, and the man, whose heart had obviously been prepared in advance, co-operated without a moment of hesitation. We may regard this as an example of the operation of God's sovereign grace, or we may think that at some earlier time Jesus had said to the man, obviously a disciple, 'I will need your help, and the use of your home one of these days.' The disciple messengers set about preparing for the Passover celebration and did not return to the group. This meant, of course, that Judas, not knowing where Jesus would be at a time when most of Jerusalem would be quiet with everyone preparing for the Passover, could take no action to tell the enemies where the upper room was. The serenity of Jesus must have contrasted greatly with the inward restlessness of Judas. Keep in mind the build up of atmosphere. This was the great feast of Passover, a reminder of the night in Egypt when the angel of judgement struck, and God's people, under the safe protection of the shed blood of the appointed lamb, were kept and delivered from their bondage and slavery (Exod. 12:1-14). Still in some places in Scotland the preparation for Communion Sunday is a solemn and sacred religious exercise. In Jerusalem that night there was an awareness of God, of his presence with and his work of salvation for his people. It was in that atmosphere that Jesus instituted the Lord's Supper. We are indeed on holy ground.

One of you...

Read also Mark 8:27-33; 1 Corinthians 10:11-13

The Passover Feast was an occasion to remember the great salvation God had worked for his people. As they ate the feast, the people were testifying that their trust and hope were in God; that they were ready to go forward with God; and that all the provision they needed came from God. Our emphasis is the same when we gather at the Lord's Table to remember him and all he has done for us. Try to imagine the atmosphere and reaction in such a situation if the Lord said to us, sitting close by him at the Table, 'One of you will betray me.' One after the other, the disciples began to say in great sorrow, 'Is it I?' Perhaps then all their earlier slowness to believe and their ambition to be first came flooding back into their minds. Their reaction to Jesus' statement seems to indicate their awareness that they could possibly do such a terrible thing. It is devastating to discover just how treacherous our fallen human nature can be and how, especially if hurt, we can lash out in word and action against those we love, respect and value. On the other hand, it could be that the disciples spoke in protest at the thought that any one of them should ever do such a thing. It seems impossible, yet appallingly possible, that even Judas asked the question! Did Peter, and the others, recall the rebuke in Mark 8:33? Had any of them ever considered the possibility that *they* might do the devil's work? How well do we know ourselves? In a given set of circumstances, how would we react? Few of us take kindly to our spirituality and dependability being questioned! Read 1 Corinthians 10:12. Soon Jesus would say a disturbing thing to Peter (Luke 22:31). The last verse of today's passage is solemn, urging us to take heed to ourselves. But it also says clearly that all is in God's perfect control.

The last supper

Read also Exodus 12:11-27

Jesus' words and actions are set in the context of the traditional Jewish celebration of the Passover, which was a family meal (see Exod. 12:11-27). At one point the head of the family would break the unleavened bread and pass a piece to each person, reminding them of the bread of affliction they ate in Egypt. It would be eaten in silence, but on this occasion Jesus spoke. He said that the bread signified his body that was to be broken to be for his people the bread of life, to nourish and sustain them on the journey of salvation. Read John 6:30-35,41-42,47-59. Throughout the Passover meal Psalms 115-118 would be sung, and towards the end of the meal another cup would be passed round. Jesus explained that this cup represented the blood of the new covenant, his blood that would be shed. *He* was the true Passover Lamb, God's Lamb, promised and foreshadowed in the Old Testament and now to be slain once for all, to seal the salvation of God's people (Heb. 7:27; 1 Cor. 5:7). Read Luke 9:31, which tells of Moses and Elijah speaking of the departure, the death, the 'exodus' he was to accomplish at Jerusalem. It is difficult to know exactly what verse 25 means, although it is clearly pointing forward beyond the cross to the victory and glory of the kingdom of God. One suggestion is that it refers to the final cup of wine at the family Passover meal, signifying the end of the occasion. If so, Jesus was indicating that his fellowship with his people was not going to be brought to an end. Indeed a whole new life and fellowship was being inaugurated. The Benediction we use at the end of a service of worship does not really signify a conclusion. We pray that grace, love and fellowship will continue to be with us, now and always, in and by the presence and power of the Holy Spirit.

The Lord's Supper

Read also John 6:30-35,48-51

After the supper, which ended with the singing of a hymn,
Jesus and his disciples (Judas having now gone, cf. John
13:21-30) went on into the next stage of God's work together.
But think again about the Lord's Supper, the Communion
Service, as we call it, the Eucharist or the Thanksgiving as
others call it. The whole emphasis is on Jesus, his person
and work, not on the symbols of bread and wine, which
remain only bread and wine. It is Jesus alone who presides
at the Table and he gives himself in unbreakable covenant
to his own. The Saviour is with his people and, as we take
and share the bread and wine, we testify by our actions
that we are taking Jesus as Saviour and Lord, and that we
seek to live and work in ongoing fellowship with him. The
emphasis is on the future. Strengthened and sustained by
the Bread of Life sent from God, we go with him into the
future, recognizing that, although our salvation is indeed
finalized and secured (Heb. 9:12, AV), there is still an un-
finished element. We follow his example in word and action, declaring his saving death and rejoicing in it until he
comes again. We do not know if it was consciously in this
spirit that the disciples followed Jesus to Gethsemane. They
may have been confused and out of their depth, as we also
may be in studying these profound verses. But they went
with Jesus. They were clear enough about that. They may
have been self-centred, arrogant, presumptuous and critical, as Peter was, but he too was clear that he was going
with Jesus. This is the right reaction to a Communion Service. At the beginning and end of such a service we should
make the words of Psalm 116:12-14 our own.

A warning

Read also Proverbs 16:18-25; 18:12-13

There is in Jesus both realism and grace. He told his disciples in the plainest of terms that they would all fall away. They would not rise to the occasion and would in fact run away. But at the same time there was no suggestion that Jesus would discard them. He spoke of his rising from the dead and how he would go before them into Galilee. It is interesting that Jesus quoted Zechariah 13:7, applying it to himself and his situation, and it is clear that in his earlier life our Lord had studied the Old Testament Scriptures. We may see here an illustration of how the Holy Spirit, the great Librarian of God's truth, brings to mind in a flash and at the right moment the very word from the Word that is needed. This shows us how important it is to store up God's Word in our minds and hearts, being attentive rather than careless, so that we are equipped for every situation as it comes. What the disciples thought of Jesus' words and to what extent they understood them we cannot tell. But Peter reacted instantly as usual and, perhaps resenting the suggestion that he would not cope, blurted out his boastful affirmation. In doing so he compared himself favourably with the others and indeed slighted them, as if hinting that he would not be surprised at their defection. Even when Jesus warned Peter about his failure, soon to come, Peter took no notice. He protested all the more vehemently, virtually saying that if Jesus was willing to die he would go with him. At this point the other disciples joined in the vows of total commitment. They were all too sure of themselves, too sure of their spiritual capacity, although their sincerity is to be commended. The devil can blind us, so that when the test comes, we are not ready. Jesus did not argue. Events not words would teach these men.

Disciples in Gethsemane

Read also Psalm 142

There is a wealth of spiritual teaching in these verses. Gethsemane was the place to which Jesus and his men went often. Judas would now know where to find them, and Jesus would know that Judas knew. The time had come. Did Jesus need his disciples to be with him, or did he take them because *they* needed to be there with him? He loved his own, right to the end (John 13:1, AV), and the safest place for them was near him. But we do not forget that Jesus was truly human and, mighty in spirit though he was, he wanted his three closest friends with him. They could not really share the burden he alone could carry, but their human presence was something he asked for. Jesus took the risk of opening his heart and telling his friends just how deeply burdened he was and he asked them for their care, their watchfulness and their empathy. He did not ask them to pray, perhaps because they would have asked for him to be spared his agony, which was impossible. Jesus just wanted their human care and compassion. He went a little further into the garden, for this was something he had to do alone, and he accepted it. When he returned to his friends he realized just how totally alone he had been. They were asleep. Did they not care? They would claim to be caring, loyal and committed to Jesus and to the work. Did they not realize that their spiritual service was simply to be awake, to be ready when Jesus wanted to talk to them and to be encouraged by their company? In verse 38 we see how Jesus cared. He was aware of Peter's danger. What kindness was in his words, 'The spirit is willing, but the body is weak.' The disciples fell asleep a second and third time. They were bewildered, weary and worn. What a contrast to their earlier words in verse 31!

Jesus in Gethsemane

Read also Galatians 3:13; 2 Corinthians 5:21; Isaiah 53:4-6

At least one of the disciples must have stayed awake for a little time, else they would not have known about Jesus falling to the ground and praying in the words recorded here. He had told them that he was troubled and burdened and, recognizing the true and full humanity of our Lord, we may say that a cloud came upon his spirit. There was no unwillingness in Jesus, no desire to turn back from the path of obedience he had trod ever since he came into the world. But there seems to have come upon his spirit an increasing awareness of the darkness and agony he was about to bear, as he was to be 'left alone with human sin', to pay its price and meet its judgement. His prayer seems to ask of his Father confirmation that this was indeed the only way, and at the same time he yielded without question to his Father's will. Jesus knew full well that very soon Judas and the soldiers would come to arrest him, and he waited for them. He did not seek to escape or to delay the crisis. The way ahead was manifestly dark, and the darkness was closing in on him. He was alone, and the way ahead would be trod alone. For that reason we must not intrude too much into this holy conversation between the Father and the Son. If we think of the symbolism of the 'scapegoat' in Leviticus 16:20-22 and how the sacrifice carrying the people's sins was led away into a desolating wilderness, we may sense something of what our Lord was aware of as he began to lay down his life for us. Isaiah 53:6 tells us that in his death God laid on him the iniquity of us all. In Gethsemane he began to feel the full weight of that load.

The traitor's kiss

Read also Matthew 26:47-50

Contrast the final serenity and assurance of Gethsemane with the tension and turmoil of this scene. Perhaps some time elapsed between the words, 'Sleep on now and take your rest,' and 'It is enough, the hour has come' (AV). If so, the picture is of Jesus the Saviour-Shepherd watching over his disciples, giving them as much rest as possible to prepare them for what was to come. Then we have Jesus' quiet assured words telling them to rise and go forward (v. 42). The agony of prayer was past. The battle had been won. Jesus was ready and waiting for the enemy to come. In verse 43 the words 'Just as he was speaking' indicate that Judas and the crowd came crashing into the garden, like a pack of mongrel dogs that feel their quarry is trapped. Today's passage begins with a vivid portrayal of Judas, one of the Twelve, the betrayer, the man who gave the treacherous kiss. Luke 22:47-48 may suggest that Jesus prevented Judas from actually kissing him, even then seeking to persuade Judas to hold back from the enormity of his crime. But Mark tells us Judas had arranged the sign of betrayal and had urged the chief priests to seize Jesus. Note the intensity of passion in Judas. He had made his decision and nothing was going to hold him back. There is something quite frightening here. It shows just how totally a man can fall into the power of the devil, even though he has kept company with Jesus and participated in Jesus' work. It is a fact of experience that few show themselves so hard and bitter in opposition to and criticism of those who are faithful to the gospel as those who have abandoned the evangelical stand they once took and rejoiced in. Beware backsliding!

The arrest

Read also John 18:2-11

They seized Jesus. We must not think of it as a formal arrest and the prisoner being told of his rights. This was a rabble, full of evil intent, and hatred is never gentle. Keep in mind the dignity and composure of Jesus. He knew the way ahead and was ready. One disciple, named later by John (John 18:10), struck out with a sword. We wonder why Peter had a sword with him in Gethsemane. Did he have it with him in the upper room as they sat at the table? Was it because he had said so publicly that regardless of what others did he would fight to the end to defend Jesus? Was Peter still thinking in merely human terms? Luke 22:36-38 may suggest this, but Jesus may have been saying, 'Enough of that kind of talk.' Had Peter not yet grasped the necessity and inevitability of the death of the Saviour? John 18:6 tells us of Jesus' powerful restraining effect and we would have imagined that this should have awed and restrained even Peter. But a powerful personality, when not yet disciplined or brought into submission to Jesus, is totally unpredictable in a crisis. John 18:11 records Jesus' words to Peter as a most gentle rebuke. It seems that Peter felt that the restraint on the soldiers signified victory, and he may have said inwardly, 'I told him his arrest and death would not happen.' Matthew 26:51-54 gives more details of Jesus' words to Peter, but it soon becomes evident that Peter still did not learn, nor did he set a guard on his own thoughts, feelings, words and actions. Of course, Peter was not the only one who failed spiritually and humanly. All the disciples fled, leaving Jesus alone. Over a spell of time they had all been more aware of their privileges than their responsibilities, and they had not built their faith on a solid enough foundation. The crisis revealed that they were not ready (14:31).

An unnamed disciple

Read also John 17:9-19

Read from verse 43 to get a full picture of the situation. The dignity, composure and control of Jesus are clear in his challenging words of rebuke, exposing the cowardly double-dealing of the Jewish leaders. If they were so sure that they were leaders of God's work, why could they not act in daylight instead of scheming behind the scenes? When people feel they have to hide what they are saying and doing there is usually something wrong. Jesus' words, 'The Scriptures must be fulfilled,' bring to mind Isaiah 53:7 or even Genesis 22:1-3,7-8. Certainly the emphasis is on God's clear and eternal plan for the salvation of his people. None of this could have been done by mere men, however evil and spiteful; only by God's sure purpose (John 19:10-11; Acts 2:23). We have noted that all the disciples fled, including Peter and an unknown young man now referred to. But who are we to criticize them, especially if we have never faced persecution? Jesus loved his followers right to the end and ensured that they were spared pressures they were not yet ready to face (John 17:9-15; 18:8-9). Now consider the young man in verses 51-52. Commentators tell us that the linen cloth garment was an expensive one and indicates someone from a wealthy family. Possibly it was Mark himself, and the upper room may have been in Mark's family home (Acts 12:12). Perhaps the crowd led by Judas had gone first to Mark's home and Mark, hearing the noise, ran on ahead to warn Jesus. Perhaps Mark followed Jesus after his arrest to see where he was taken, but the arresting party wanted neither witnesses nor spies, and the young man, his life threatened, fled. Whoever he was, in the midst of such a dark picture, it is good to see the light of youthful love in devotion to Jesus.

Are you the Christ?

Read also John 18:12-14,19-24

The scene moves to the house of the high priest. Jesus had already been cross-examined by Annas (John 18:12-14,19-24). Now the examination was by the whole Sanhedrin, which officially had very strict rules to guard against any miscarriage of justice. However, the court seems to have met unofficially because it was night-time, and what they were doing 'in the dark' would have to be made official after daybreak (Mark 15:1). The chief priests were not interested in examining evidence but looked for witnesses who would speak against Jesus. In view of the bargain the priests had struck with Judas, it is quite possible that witnesses were paid to give testimony, but in the event the various testimonies did not agree. Try to imagine the increasingly angry frustration of these evil men and in the midst of them the silent, dignified, suffering Jesus. This was not a trial, nor even an examination; it was a deliberate plot led by the accredited religious leaders of the Jews. They were blinded by their hatred, which stemmed from persistent unbelief. It was devilish. When the scheme to get an accusation that would stick failed, Caiaphas the high priest intervened. Using his position to speak with the kind of authority few would resist, he demanded that Jesus should speak and so incriminate himself. But Jesus stood silent. Think of the Lord Jesus standing in manly and regal dignity in the midst of a pack of human wolves. What an impact that silence must have had! Faced with Jesus' silence, the high priest put him under oath (Matt. 26:63) and then asked the question that lay at the heart of the whole situation. The high priest exposed exactly what he resented and what he had refused to believe. When asked, 'Are you the Christ?' Jesus said, 'I am.' Nothing could be clearer.

The trial

Read also Daniel 7:13-14; Luke 23:50-53

For three years the words and works of Jesus had testified to his identity but the religious leaders of the Jews refused to believe. Now, as they thought, they had him in their power. In answer to the question, Jesus declared himself to be the Son of Man, a term the Sanhedrin would recognize from Daniel 7:13-14, and they knew beyond doubt that Jesus was claiming to be that one who was given kingship and the right to judge by God himself. As far as the high priest was concerned he now had a confession, witnessed by the whole committee. Caiaphas' tearing of his clothes was the traditional symbol of expressing sorrow, but here it was an expression of fiendish triumph. Through fear of Caiaphas' ecclesiastical power, the vast majority of those present agreed with the evil man. Mark says that all of them condemned Jesus, which suggests that Joseph and Nicodemus were not present. Perhaps they had not been told about the meeting. Earlier Nicodemus had protested at judgement being passed on Jesus without a fair hearing, and had been savagely silenced (John 7:45-52). If Joseph of Arimathea was present when the decision was put to the vote, he refused to condemn Jesus (Luke 23:50-53). If Nicodemus and Joseph had been present Jesus would have been aware of their exercise of heart, regarding him as they did, and yet at that point not being able to do anything to prevent the situation developing. There are still situations like that, in which we have to submit, feeling helpless and even guilty, and yet constrained by the sovereign overruling of God. In verse 65 we are told of religious hatred, with all its polite camouflage thrown away. These were the orthodox, supposedly balanced, intellectual religious people dealing with the 'fundamentalist' Jesus.

Peter's folly

Read also 1 Peter 3:15-17; 5:6-8

Peter had followed Jesus at a distance right into the court-yard of the high priest (v. 54), having enlisted the help of John in order to get in (John 18:15-16). If we are tempted to criticize Peter, remember the situation and atmosphere of open, bitter and apparently successful hatred and rejection of Jesus. Although he may not have been aware of it, Peter was under deliberate attack from the devil. Instead of being so determined to be 'near the action' it would have been better for Peter to have gone away quietly to ponder how often he had said and done the wrong things, and how Jesus had warned him of the dangers of that very night (Mark 14:29-31). He should have been aware of the evil one (Luke 22:31). Perhaps his own emotional and spiritual confusion made him insensitive to spiritual danger. He had blundered on (v. 54), drawn or driven by his affection and regard for Jesus, and perhaps ashamed of having fallen asleep in Gethsemane and of his bravado with the sword (v. 47). There had been opportunity for him to get away from the crowded courtyard when he made his way to the gate (Mark 14:68), but he hesitated. Those who spoke to Peter were not necessarily challenging him in an antagonistic way. They may have wanted to ask questions and hear first-hand news. If so, Peter had an opportunity to witness that he failed to take, and we should note his words in 1 Peter 3:15-17. Peter had not been ready. In verse 68 he said, 'I don't know what you are talking about.' In the next verse possibly the same maid, perhaps serving a group of men who were discussing Jesus, drew their attention to Peter. But again Peter denied knowing Jesus. At some time after the first or second encounter a cock must have crowed (v. 72), but Peter took no notice of the warning. He denied his Lord a third time.

Peter wept

Read also Acts 2:22-24,36-40; 4:8-12

All four Gospels record this event, which indicates its importance, especially for all those who tend to be too sure of their understanding, their commitment and their spirituality (Matt. 26:69-75; Luke 22:56-62; John 18:16-18,25-27). The first three Gospels record that in the crisis moment, just too late, Peter remembered what Jesus had said, and wept. Only Luke records that at the moment of denial the Lord turned and looked at Peter. In the midst of all the pressure, threatening, contempt and imminent suffering, Jesus thought of his disciple Peter. We can only imagine the look of exquisite care, pity and love that shone from the eyes of the Saviour. We can only imagine the compassionate prayer that rose from his heart for his broken disciple, over whom the waves of shame were already breaking. Of course, all that wonderful love shining from Jesus' eyes would have been missed if Peter had not been looking to Jesus at that precise moment. The fact that he did so, in the very moment of his failure, tells us a lot about Peter. We can understand his tears. Tears can be a good sign, provided they are not just self-pity (2 Cor. 7:8-11). How kind Jesus is to those who fall! Many have proved it. The whole story of Peter shows his greatness and his weakness, his spirituality and his blindness. We have seen this at Caesarea Philippi (Mark 8:27-33). We see his spiritual leadership in the early chapters of Acts, then arguing with God in Acts 10:13-16. We see his amazing faith and trust as he slept in prison, facing death, in Acts 12:6. In Galatians 2:11-13 he is rebuked for his uncertainty and hesitation, blurring the truth of the gospel. Yes, Peter blundered and denied his Lord, but out of the furnace of affliction came the true man. Of course, his wonderful Saviour was praying for him (Luke 22:31-32).

Pilate's trial

Read also John 18:33-38

The Sanhedrin met formally in the morning in order to regularize the decisions of the night-time meeting. The enemies of Jesus were not going to let him out of their power because of a legal or procedural technicality. They resolved to have Jesus put to death, but such a sentence could only be carried out by the Roman authorities. This execution they were determined to secure, whatever the method or the cost. Their minds had been made up for a long time, as Mark 3:6 and 14:1 make plain. Imagine the accusers, hard-faced, inflexible, their looks of triumph scarcely hidden, and imagine ruthless, weak Pilate, as this crowd bore down on his official residence. It is a grim picture. When dealing with the devil, or with people influenced consciously or unconsciously by the devil, we need to be careful, to weigh their words, and so discern their motives. Jesus was handed over to Pilate, perhaps along with a written minute of the Sanhedrin meeting, declaring that by unanimous decision Jesus had been found deserving of death. There was no love lost between the Jews and the governor, and Pilate started proceedings by asking a political question. If Jesus claimed to be a king, then Rome would consider the charge of treason against the state. Possibly this was the accusation the Jews put forward, feeling that their main charge of blasphemy would not impress Pilate. If Pilate's word 'you' is emphasized we can see his mockery. Jesus answered in the affirmative. Read John 18:33-38 for a fuller account of the interview.

The silent Jesus

Read also John 19:1-16

In Mark's brief but powerful account of proceedings, verse 3 indicates that some considerable time was taken up with the chief priest's accusations, which, however confused and repetitive, had to be considered by Pilate as he heard the case. His sense of Roman justice may have caused him to refer each accusation to Jesus for him to defend himself. But the governor was totally baffled by Jesus' silence. Of course, the decision about the cross had been made in heaven's courtroom and nothing could now delay, let alone avert it. Pilate had no understanding of that and, as John 19:1-16 makes plain, he schemed, compromised by scourging Jesus, appealed to the human decency of the crowd (vv. 4-5), and then tried to pass the problem on to Herod, without success. Still Jesus remained silent. At length Pilate seems to have become angry and he spoke the words of John 19:10-11 sternly, and with as much authority as he could then muster. The answer Jesus gave frightened him, but the frenzied hatred of the chief priests frightened him even more. Their implied threat to report his weakness to Caesar finally decided him (John 19:15). Pilate's administration had already caused him problems with his masters in Rome and, being a politician more concerned with his position than with moral and spiritual issues, he took what he thought was the obvious course. He delivered Jesus into the hands of the chief priests. Pilate had already declared publicly that Jesus had done no wrong and that Herod had come to the same conclusion (Luke 23:14-15). Godless political power was making it clear that this innocent man was going to die for sins that were not his own.

The power of the mob

Read also Acts 19:21-34

It was a Roman custom, as a gesture to a subject people, to release some convicted prisoner whom the Jews requested. This had become so established that, according to Luke 23:17 (AV and footnote in NIV), Pilate felt he had to comply. There was a notorious murderer whose guilt was not in question, reportedly called Jesus Barabbas. By now there was a crowd, possibly gathered by the priests and scribes, and certainly incited by them, resulting in an intense popular demonstration. The crowd may have essentially been against the political power of Rome, rather than against Jesus, but a crowd can so easily be manipulated, especially when feelings are running high, as they certainly were at the time of the Passover Feast. We would like to think that this was a totally different crowd from the one that shouted 'Hosanna!' on Palm Sunday, but religious excitement is not very dependable, nor very discerning of spiritual truth. Pilate's words in verses 9-10 seem to come from a mixture of contempt and bravado, but they had no effect in the face of a crowd already chanting their mindless slogans. In modern terms the shouts would be 'We want Barabbas!' and 'Crucify, crucify, crucify!' In that atmosphere Pilate's question in verse 14 would have gone completely unheard. The people may not have been aware of it, but the whole situation was totally evil. Did even the chief priests realize that they were in the process of crucifying the Lord of glory (1 Cor. 2:8)? We may criticize Pilate, but how often have we been swayed by the attitude and atmosphere of a particular unbelieving crowd? Pilate's question in verse 12, differently worded in Matthew 27:22, is one we all have to face and answer. Pilate's answer was fatal for him. The chief priests stood by their choice. We will all be judged by our answer.

The crown of thorns

Read also Acts 3:13-15; Hebrews 12:15-17

The soldiers, under command of Roman officers and responsible for carrying out the sentence of crucifixion, led Jesus away inside the governor's headquarters. The whole battalion was gathered, ready for 'sport' with the victim. Although Pilate had not given orders for the torment that followed, he had earlier ordered the scourging of Jesus, and we are reluctant even to think of the suffering our Lord endured. Pilate would have heard the noise and would have known what was happening, but by now his own weakness had made him powerless to prevent it. Acts 3:13 indicates the pressure on Pilate's conscience. He had decided to release Jesus, but did not do so. History tells us that his political career very soon ended in disgrace. Dare we hope that the remorse he must have felt as he listened to the ribaldry of the soldiers led him to an awareness of his own sinfulness? Other evil men have found a place of repentance. Of course, some calculating men and women, for human advancement, have sold out spiritually and have ended like Esau, who wept but found no place of repentance (Heb. 12:15-17, AV). Mark 14:65 tells us the religious authorities mocked Jesus as God's Prophet. Now the secular powers mocked his claim to be King. Having been virtually stripped for scourging, Jesus was 'dressed up' in a purple cloak, the royal colour. A crown made of hideous thorns was pressed on to his head and, according to Matthew 27:29, they put a reed into his hand as a mocking royal sceptre. Then, having shown their contempt for Jesus' claim to be a king, they stripped him of his 'royal regalia', reducing him in their sight to be a mere man again, a criminal to be executed. The Son of God was totally devalued, and we are only at the beginning of the price paid for our salvation.

Carrying the cross

Read also Philippians 2:5-8; Mark 8:34-38

We are in the middle of a great crowd, noisy, curious, indifferent, but with many gloating with pleasure that this man was on his way to humiliating death as a public spectacle. There were also those who were deeply upset (Luke 23:27-28). The events leading up to this have revealed what religious, and secular, human nature is capable of. If people could do this to the sinless, gentle, good, manly Jesus, we should not be surprised by the atrocities of our own day. Surrounded by a guard of soldiers, Jesus had forfeited all his rights and was in the process of humbling himself to death, even the death of the cross (Phil. 2:5-8). John 19:17 tells us that Jesus carried his own cross but, when he staggered with exhaustion, the soldiers commandeered Simon of Cyrene to carry the load. There is no suggestion that the soldiers did this out of compassion, although we would not be surprised if some stirring of humanity resulted from the sight of the Saviour. We can be sure that the Holy Spirit was working actively in every development of these events. Mark makes a point of referring to Simon's two sons, which suggests they were well known in the church by the time Mark was writing his record of the gospel. There is reference to Rufus in Romans 16:13, and to his mother as a well-loved Christian friend of Paul. Simon was probably in Jerusalem for the Passover. He was compelled to carry the cross, but it seems that the experience of that and the events at the crucifixion had a profound effect on him. Imagine him telling his wife and sons about Jesus, saying, 'I carried his cross'; and of Jesus calling his disciples to take up the cross and follow him (Mark 8:34-35). Simon had heard the mockery of the crowd. He knew what it would mean to follow Jesus. He had counted the cost. So must we.

Golgotha

Read also Luke 4:1-13

The brevity of Mark's account makes the event all the more stark. Executions were carried out in a public place, perhaps as a warning to evildoers. When they came to Golgotha, Jesus was offered a drink, which was a drug intended to deaden the pain of crucifixion. We do not know if the soldiers offered the drink or if it was some compassionate person in the crowd. The drug was refused because Jesus was to yield his life in full consciousness, and everything that had yet to be spoken was to be voiced with clarity and assurance, so that it could not be mistaken. The whole kingdom of sin and Satan was about to be dealt with fully and finally, and Jesus needed a clear mind and spirit in order to discern and reject the last attempts of the devil to frustrate this glorious work of salvation. Remember the activity of Satan at the time of Jesus' birth, especially the murderous fury of Herod (Matt. 2:16). Remember Satan's intense assault, when he tempted Jesus right at the start of his ministry (Luke 4:1-13). Throughout his work, Jesus was resisted by Satan, not only through his critics, but also through the misguided feelings of friends such as Peter (Mark 8:31-33). Who but Satan lay behind the agony in Gethsemane? We will soon read of Satan's subtle temptation in the midst of our Lord's suffering, as voices promised to believe and to follow if only he would come down from the cross. People still want Christianity without the cross because the cross, beyond any shadow of doubt, declares that all are sinners and need a Saviour. It calls all to a life of obedient, self-denying sacrifice. Wherever and whenever 'Jesus Christ and him crucified' is preached (1 Cor. 2:2) the devil will be present to oppose and distract. We need to watch and pray. It will not be easy. It was not easy for Jesus.

The crucifixion

Read also Psalm 22:1,6-8,14-18

They crucified him. Some enjoyed what they saw as their victory. The soldiers were indifferent, concerned only with their rights to share the victim's clothing. Recognizing the value of the seamless outer garment, they gambled for it (John 19:23-24). No doubt Jesus, seeing and hearing what was going on, would recall Psalm 22:16-18. That same psalm will echo again and again as we read on through the story of the death of the Son of God. Mark records the fact very simply: they crucified him. But we must not see this as merely the work of evil men nor even the work of the devil. Read Acts 2:22-23; 4:27-28. It was God who spared not even his own Son but delivered him up for us all (John 3:16; Rom. 8:32). In Matthew 27:36 (AV) we read, 'And sitting down they watched him there.' No doubt the words refer to the soldiers who would have claimed that they were only obeying orders. The officer in charge was eventually moved deeply, perhaps even to faith. Whether others were similarly affected we cannot tell, but the preaching of the cross, even when it carries the unmistakable unction of the Holy Spirit, still leaves many totally unmoved. It has always been so, and will be until the end, for even when Christ comes again in his glory there will still be those who choose to remain in their unbelief (1 Cor. 1:18; Rev. 1:7; 16:9,11). The inscription on the cross, which was the accusation against him, read, 'The King of the Jews'. The full title, the resentment of the chief priests, and Pilate's contemptuous retort are recorded in John 19:19-22. Did Pilate's refusal to change the wording indicate that already he knew in measure the terrible thing he had done, which has caused the words 'Crucified under Pontius Pilate' to be witnessed against him down the course of history?

The dying thieves

Read also Luke 23:33-43

In the NIV verse 28 is inserted as a footnote: 'And the scripture was fulfilled . . . and he was numbered with the transgressors' (Isa. 53:9,12; cf. Luke 22:37). Jesus died between two criminals. But Jesus' guilt was not his own. He died 'the righteous for the unrighteous', the guiltless for the guilty, to bring us to God (1 Peter 3:18). Luke 23:33-43 gives the full picture of the thieves, suggesting that Jesus' wonderful words, 'Father forgive them', were heard by the thieves and awakened in one of them his plea for mercy. It is important to note in Luke's account that these words were spoken in a situation and atmosphere of total mockery, contempt, unbelief and bitterness; yet they brought the response of faith from a most unlikely convert who had left the issue of the salvation of his soul to the very last moment. Mark's one verse portrays Jesus in his death as he was in his life, found among the sinners he had come to seek and to save. But we must see how the light of the cross exposes as well as saves. The first thief, with no trace of regret let alone repentance, snarled, 'If you really are God, get us out of this mess.' He wanted a God to 'get him off the hook', no doubt to go back to his former way of life. There was no sense of sin, no desire to change, just bitterness against man and God because his evil life had caught up with him. The second thief recognized the justice of his condemnation, the rightness of the judgement, and the fact that Jesus had done nothing deserving of death. He saw, very faintly perhaps, that Jesus was not dying for his own sins and that he must be dying for others. Two men were at the end of bad, sinful lives and faced the penalty. One believed and was saved: no one need despair. Only one was saved: no one may presume.

Indifference

Read also Lamentations 1:12; 3:13-15

Verses such as these should keep us from ever thinking
sentimentally about the crucifixion. Imagine what it must
have been like to be there and think how desperately hard
it must have been for anyone to speak a word of witness in
favour of Jesus. Those who passed by in the busy public
place shouted out the contemptuous words of mockery,
perhaps having asked the priests and scribes what was going
on. These devil-inspired religious hypocrites may not have
done the actual shouting (having regard for their reputa-
tions) but they saw to it that the utmost derision was thrown
at the suffering Son of God. There was a crowd there,
gathered to see the 'show', and they may have enjoyed the
mockery of those who saw such little significance in what
was happening that they simply walked on. The phrase
'passed by' (Lam. 1:12) describes the attitude of so many, to
this very day. On the cross, the heart of God in redeeming
love is fully exposed, but it scarcely merits a passing glance.
We must also see in verse 29 the contemptuous rejection of
Jesus' ministry, because the reference is to the words spoken
by him in the temple precincts as recorded in Mark 13:1-2ff,
and referred to in Jesus' examination before Caiaphas (Mark
14:58). Read Psalm 22:1,6-8 and Lamentations 1:12 again,
Scriptures that would have been well known to our Lord.
No one who stands in the presence of the cross and speaks
with derision like this can possibly be of God. The cross is
very searching! But all they were saying and doing was
known to God and on the great day of judgement they shall
answer to God. Keep that solemn thought in mind when
next you hear anyone, especially religious 'leaders' (who
are they leading?), speaking with derision and unbelief
about the death of the Son of God.

He saved others

Read also John 10:11-18; 19:7-11

The ecclesiastical hypocrites, no doubt fully robed, would soon take a prominent public part in the celebration of the Passover, but amongst themselves they mocked everything about the Saviour. Rejoicing in what they saw as their victory, they made fun of him, but in their bitter words they spoke profound truth. They bore testimony to the reality of Jesus' ministry of word and power, acknowledging that he had saved others. Countless lives bore unmistakable testimony to the saving, transforming and liberating power of Jesus Christ, the Son of God. But in order to save sinners he could not save himself. Jesus was taking the sinner's place, dying the sinner's death. This had been determined in eternity before ever he was born in Bethlehem. He came to save his people from their sins (Matt. 1:21). He took his stand with sinners when he was baptized in Jordan (Mark 1:9-11). When the time came, he set his face to go to Jerusalem (Luke 9:51). In Gethsemane he again confirmed his willingness to do the work he had come to do (Mark 14:36), and he made plain to Pilate that his life was not being taken from him: he was giving it up freely (John 10:18; 19:10-11). He endured the cross for the joy set before him, the joy of saving his people everlastingly (Heb. 12:2). Jesus' enemies were right about his death. It was a substitutionary death. He took the place of the sinner. What if Jesus had answered their challenge and come down from the cross? The dying thief would have been left without a Saviour. The people, including the wicked priests, would have been faced with their Judge. 'Come down from the cross!' is still the cry of many religious people, because the cross declares that all are sinners and need a Saviour. It is our attitude to the cross that exposes whether we are of God or not (1 Cor. 1:18).

Darkness at the cross

Read also Matthew 27:45-50; Luke 23:44-49

These verses, so simple and yet so gripping, take us right to the heart of the cross where the Son of God died. Matthew 27:45-50 and Luke 23:44-49 add details to complete the picture. Of course, it is not the *story* of the cross that constitutes the gospel. As a story it is grim and depressing, the story of the best man who ever lived being put to death by callous religious hypocrites. It is the message or theology of the cross that is the gospel, and we must seek to grasp the significance of what was happening. Sin was being dealt with and the whole kingdom of evil was being challenged and conquered, once for all (Col. 2:13-15; Heb. 9:24-28; 1 Peter 3:18). It was the third hour when Jesus had been crucified (Mark 15:25). Now it was the sixth hour, and a great darkness covered the whole scene until the ninth hour. It was a supernatural darkness but, even if it impressed some people at the time, we see later that the chief priests and others were not changed by it and their bitter unbelief persisted. What did the darkness signify? Did it symbolize the judgement of God falling upon sin? That would help us in measure to understand the terrible cry, 'My God, my God, why hast Thou forsaken me?' The sin-bearer was 'left alone with human sin' (John Ellerton) to pay its price and meet its judgement, which meant separation from God. The Saviour really paid the price of sin. He went into darkness so that *we* would not go there. The darkness may also signify that God hid this crucial moment of atonement, so that none but the Father and the Son might know what it cost to work salvation for sinners. Such thoughts should help us to sing, 'When I survey the wondrous Cross,' and to worship when we sing Wesley's words, 'Amazing love! how can it be that thou, my God, shouldst die for me?'

Words from the cross

Read also Romans 5:6-11; Galatians 3:13

Throughout the three hours of darkness five of the seven 'Words from the cross' were spoken. The words, 'Father forgive them,' were spoken before the words to the dying thief, 'Today you will be with me in paradise' (Luke 23:34,43). In the midst of his agony, John 19:25-27 records the Saviour's kind words to his mother and to the disciple John. It is astonishing that such a tender human note should be sounded in such a horrifying context. Such a family bond created by redeeming love teaches us a great deal about Christian duty to care for one another. The hearts of those who heard this must have been touched very deeply. We have already spoken of the cry, 'My God, why hast Thou forsaken Me?' It was a cry of dereliction and reminds us of the testimony of 2 Corinthians 5:21: 'God made him who had no sin to be sin for us.' He was identified with sin, so much so that the face of the Father was hidden. Our inability to understand this signifies how little we understand the sinfulness of sin, God's rejection of it and his judgement on it (Hab. 1:13). The only personal word from the cross was 'I am thirsty' (John 19:28; cf. Ps. 22:14-15) and this was spoken when Jesus knew his work was finished. It was not an appeal for sympathy, but a request to quench his thirst before his next triumphal statement, 'It is finished!' (John 19:30). The whole plan of salvation had been completed. God's Man, our Man, who came to earth for us, who had lived for us, now has died for us. Mark simply refers to a loud cry and then Jesus breathed his last. Luke 23:46 records the assured faith of the Saviour as he committed himself to the Father, and Matthew 27:50 tells how the Saviour yielded, or dismissed his spirit. The end was the victory of one who knew his work was completed.

Those who watched

Read also Matthew 27:51-54; Acts 7:51 - 8:1

When the mighty work of salvation was being brought to its glorious, triumphant conclusion, some of the bystanders, possibly mistaking Jesus' cry, 'Eloi, Eloi', for a reference to Elijah, may have looked for some last-minute arrival of the prophet to deliver Jesus from death. Some were compassionate and offered Jesus a drink, but others preferred to wait for a possible miracle. They had no idea of the mighty work that was being done before their eyes. It is a common tragedy. So often when God is at work, we are not aware of it. Perhaps it is because we have not taken seriously what we have been taught. Perhaps it is because we are too self-centred. When Jesus died, the curtain in the temple, which symbolized that the way into God's presence was closed, was torn from top to bottom. Did those who witnessed this and those who heard of it later realize what it meant? Were they thrilled that there was now a way opened for sinners to come to God? The scene was certainly set for the preaching of the gospel. But one man was profoundly moved by all that he had seen and heard at the place called Calvary, and that was the Roman centurion. Whether he said, 'This was *a* son of God,' or 'This was *the* Son of God,' we cannot be sure. He certainly knew Jesus was no ordinary man and that his was no ordinary death. He could see that somehow this death was not a defeat but a victory. The centurion had stood facing Jesus as he died, and he and the soldiers were filled with awe (Matt. 27:54). Even the crowd was troubled, no doubt wondering about the earthquake coinciding with Jesus' death (Luke 23:48). Then came the Sabbath. God's work was complete and the Father and the Son rested from their labours. The work of the Holy Spirit was to prepare the people for resurrection day.

What did it mean?

Read also Colossians 1:19-23; 2:13-15

The women were there right to the end. It happens so often. After the men, who may have been so sure of their spirituality, have gone, the women are still there. Mark does not mention our Lord's mother and perhaps by this time John had taken Mary away from the agonizing sight of Jesus' last moments, although this is unlikely. These women had followed Jesus and ministered to him and to the disciples. Such consistency of faith and commitment was not likely to wither at the most critical stage. Perhaps they had believed more truly than the men what Jesus had taught so often about the necessity of his death. To what extent at this stage they understood the full significance of that atoning death we cannot tell. But in due time they would be taught by the apostles in great detail the full, glorious meaning. It is recorded in Scripture for all time. God so loved the world that he gave his Son, and sparing him not, he gave him up for us (John 3:16; Rom. 5:8; 8:32). God was in Christ reconciling the world to himself, not reckoning our trespasses against us (2 Cor. 5:19-20). God sent his Son to redeem us, to buy us back from sinful bondage (Gal. 4:4-5), and through him God made peace for sinners through the blood of the cross (Col. 1:20), taking away the catalogue of sin that stood against us and breaking the power of evil (Col. 2:13-15). When the Son of God had, by himself, made purification for (or had purged) our sins, he sat down at the right hand of God (Heb. 1:1-3). The work of salvation was complete, but we must never forget its cost (1 Peter 1:18-20). The cross is indeed wondrous, and it demands our surrender and service. The devotion and dedication of these women is put on record. There was nothing they could do, but they were there, and Jesus would have known it.

Courage in crisis

Read also John 19:31-42

Jesus died at three in the afternoon (the ninth hour) which, in Jewish reckoning, was the beginning of the 'evening'. The Sabbath, our Saturday, was calculated as starting at six o'clock on Friday, and from that time no Jew would do any work at all. The Sanhedrin would have known, as all others would have known, the regulation in Deuteronomy 21:22-23 about the bodies of those punished by death having to be taken down before night. It was Joseph of Arimathea, assisted by Nicodemus (John 19:38-42), who realized there were only three hours left before the Sabbath to deal with the burial of Jesus and he acted quickly, so quickly that Pilate was amazed that Jesus was already dead. John's account (John 19:31-37) gives harrowing details, which also indicate that the Sanhedrin had taken note of the Sabbath regulations. These details show that Pilate must have been disturbed by the fact that Jesus had not died in the 'normal' way of a criminal execution. We cannot believe that Joseph acted only or primarily from a concern for the sanctity of the Sabbath. In his going to Pilate, we must note his courage, because as a respected member of the Sanhedrin he was coming out into the open as a man who had, in measure at least, come to a love for and faith in Jesus Christ. His courage was not in facing Pilate but in risking the wrath and ostracism of the high priests. We are told that Joseph was looking for the kingdom of God, just as old Simeon and Anna had been at the beginning of the story in Luke 2:25-32. Just as Simeon had at a certain point 'seen' the truth, so Joseph seems to have come to faith at some point during the awe-ful events of that first Good Friday.

The burial

Read also Hebrews 1:1-3; 3:12-15

Mark speaks of the women as well as Joseph and how concerned they were with the 'last things' they could do for their Master. Joseph asked for the body for burial and the women noted where the grave was, so that they could carry out the normal anointing of the body after the Sabbath. They had witnessed the tragedy of the death of Jesus, whom they had come to trust and love. We cannot tell just how much they understood of the meaning of the cross, nor what, if anything, they expected to happen next. The events of the first Easter day certainly took them by surprise. Having witnessed the crucifixion, sensed the dark and terrible atmosphere, heard the words from the cross, and no doubt recalled some of what they had heard of Jesus' teaching, the women and Joseph were constrained to respond. Their hearts may have yielded to Jesus long before, but now they had the opportunity to do something that both expressed and confirmed their faith. It was still tentative faith, very limited in understanding, but at a time when all the 'front-line' disciples had fled, these few came out into the open. On the face of it, the events of the cross had dashed their hopes. Having heard Jesus' cry, 'My God, why ...?' no doubt they too were crying from aching hearts, 'Why had it to happen? What did it mean? Why did God allow it?' And yet they responded. Their hearts had been moved and won even though their understanding was so very limited. Here is a lesson for all engaged in the work of the gospel. We may not demand full understanding and exact doctrinal consent before we accept someone as a believer. Of course, the proof of real faith is that it will respond gladly and eagerly to the truth as it becomes ever more clear. True faith will always hunger for teaching.

A desolate Saturday

Read also Luke 24:13-24

We will never understand the amazement, the surging of
mixed emotions, the mingling of unbelief and joy in the
disciples on the day of resurrection if we do not first ponder the bleak desolation and fear of the Sabbath day. There
was nothing they could do and nowhere they could go.
Wherever they were at the beginning of the Sabbath, there
they had to stay. We must not think of a large company of
Jesus' disciples all being together, sharing the comfort and
support that fellowship can give. Families would be together
for the Passover, but there could have been Jewish homes
where only one person had any real regard for or trust in
Jesus. Try to imagine how depressed and disappointed many
of his followers would have been at the way things had
worked out. Would they have been thinking over some of
his teachings, searching for some understanding of what
he had said so often about his death, and what it meant
when he spoke of being raised up (Matt. 16:21)? Luke's account of the disciples on the road to Emmaus (Luke
24:13-24) indicates their total lack of expectation and their
fairly swift adjustment to life without Jesus. It is almost an
invasion of privacy for us to ask what Peter's thoughts and
feelings were. He had promised so much, so publicly. He
would not have found it easy to be a public failure. But no
doubt his deepest hurt would have been, 'What would Jesus
think of me now? What future can there be for a failure?'
Peter may well have found shelter in the home of John, just
as Mary the mother of our Lord had done (John 20:2; 19:26-
27). Some of the women would have been discussing the
arrangements for the visit to the grave after the Sabbath.
There was no thought of a joyous resurrection day; but the
light was about to shine.

The stone rolled away

Read also Matthew 28:1-15

The story is wonderful in its simplicity, humanity and power. If you have time, read the fuller and varied accounts in Matthew 28, Luke 24, and John 20 and 21. Even though the story is familiar it will shed fresh light. It always does, and we cannot read the facts too often. Mark tells us that the women saw a problem. Who would move the stone, the only barrier to their carrying out this service of love to the Master they thought dead? But God was ahead of them. The stone was removed. The way to their service ordained by God was made open for them. Mark does not mention any earthquake, nor the guard of soldiers set to prevent any organized stealing of the body, nor the scheming lies by which Jesus' enemies tried to deny the fact of the resurrection (Matt. 27:62-66; 28:12-15). Mark wrote his account early and simply emphasizes the basic and glorious fact that the tomb was empty. Note that the event of the resurrection was every bit as quiet and out of the public eye as the birth of the Saviour in Bethlehem had been. The women went into the tomb, which was really a small cave hewn out of the rock (Matt. 27:59-60). A man dressed in white, obviously an angel, spoke to them, telling them not to be alarmed, which very naturally they were. The removal of the stone had taken them by surprise and they would have assumed it was done by the gardener who looked after the place (John 20:15). They were astonished at seeing an angel, as all of us would be. Then the angel spoke to them, indicating that he knew why they were there. We must not make the characters in the biblical story into superhuman beings. They were just like us, and their reactions in verse 8 were every bit as 'non-spiritual' and illogical as ours often are.

The first witnesses

Read also Luke 24:9-11,22-24

What a wonderful encouragement there is in this simple account of the resurrection. These very human women, bewildered and quite frightened, were in fact the first persons to be entrusted with the announcement of the Resurrection Gospel. This is quite astonishing when we remember that in those days women, being regarded as second-class citizens, were not acceptable as witnesses in a court case. If, as some suggest, the resurrection was a fictional story to perpetuate the memory of Jesus, rather than a historical fact, the fraudsters would never have given such a prominent role to women. These women knew full well that Jesus had been crucified. They knew where he had been buried. They did not need an angel to tell them of these facts. But think of their reaction to the words, 'He is risen; he is not here.' If the women had been capable of saying anything, they would probably have asked, 'Where is he?' The answer to that, of course, is that he is everywhere. He is with us, alive for evermore. But before the women could really think what it all meant, they were commissioned by this heavenly messenger to go and tell the disciples. Again, there must have been the inward reaction, 'But they won't believe it. They won't listen to women.' That reaction was right on target, as Luke 24:9-11,22-24 makes plain. Men, especially those who assume they are spiritually superior, can be very stupid at times. But we must give credit to John and Peter, two very different characters, perhaps of different age groups, and in very different mental and emotional states after the crucifixion, because they listened to the women and then went to the grave (John 20:1-9). At least *they* were thinking what it could mean if Jesus really was raised from the dead.

Tell Peter

Read also John 21:15-23

The angel made special mention of the fact that Peter had to be told that Jesus was alive from the dead. Peter would no doubt react with a mighty surge of hope, followed by a plunge into desolation. Why would Jesus want him after his miserable denial? Did he fear a public rebuke and a notice of redundancy? Jesus did want him and had plans for his lifetime of service, but there were things to be spoken about. We are told in 1 Corinthians 15:5 of a personal and private appearance of Jesus to Peter, and that shows us something of the immense kindness of Jesus in dealing with a fallen disciple in the interest of his restoration. In John 21 we are given a much more detailed account, revealing some of the deep flaws in Peter's personality and showing how very little he had changed from how he had been before the cross. Of course Paul's letter to the Corinthians was written possibly thirty years before John wrote his Gospel. By the time John was writing, Peter's mighty ministry from Pentecost onwards was well known and the details John gave would not reflect darkly on Peter as a Christian leader. Rather, it would be an encouragement to many Christians who were suffering, and especially those who had failed during persecution. It would make them realize that failures and blunders do not automatically disqualify a Christian from service. It is important to remember that the risen Christ, in all the glory of his person, victory and exaltation, is no less understanding than the Jesus we have read about right through Mark's story of his life. Read the Scottish paraphrase, 'Where high the heavenly temple stands,' and remember that the risen, glorified Christ still knows, understands and feels for us in all our human experiences. This is the Saviour who goes before us and with us.

Mary Magdalene

Read also John 20:1-18

The NIV draws a line after verse 8 and states categorically
that the most reliable early manuscripts do not have verses
9-20. Most other translations indicate less forcefully that
some manuscripts have the passage but others do not. Most
versions actually print the verses, which indicates that although they may not originally be part of Mark's Gospel
they are still authentic. Some suggest the original manu-
script on which Mark wrote was mutilated at an early stage,
and later, when the Gospels of Matthew and Luke were
written, a compilation of resurrection incidents was added
to Mark to complete the account. Others suggest Mark was
prevented from completing his story because of persecution. It seems best to study these verses, being cautious
only where single statements seem to be out of harmony
with the other Gospels. Some commentators suggest that
John 21 preserves part, or even all, of what is called the
'lost' ending of Mark's Gospel. Certainly, if we were to end
at verse 8, it would seem an abrupt and unsatisfactory ending to a dynamically written story. The verses we read today
tell of Jesus appearing to Mary Magdalene, whom he had
gloriously delivered from the power and possession of seven
demons (Luke 8:2). John 20:1-2,11-18 fills out the touching
details of this appearance. We can understand Mary's distress, made worse by the fear that these evil spirits might
return to dominate her life (Matt. 12:43-45). Think what it
must have meant to her to recognize his voice speaking her
name. Reassured by Jesus, she went instantly to tell the
weeping disciples, but they would not believe her. That
must have been a devastating blow to someone who owed
so much to Jesus and who loved him genuinely and trusted
his word. Gratitude and obedience usually go together.

Meeting Jesus

Read also John 21:1-14

The story of Mary Magdalene is set on the morning of the first Easter day, and the story of the road to Emmaus deals with the afternoon and evening of that day (Luke 24:13-35). Luke also tells us that the Lord had appeared to Peter. Both Mark and Luke record the fact of the disciples' unbelief. No matter how often they had been told by Jesus that he would die, and rise again on the third day, they still could not believe it when it happened. This is one reason why we should never be weary of being told the same truths over and over again. We need the Word of God to impress the truth on our minds and hearts, so that no matter how our immediate circumstances change, no matter how many unexpected things happen to us, no matter in what way we meet the risen Jesus, we will at once recognize who he is and what his presence means in terms of total victory over the world, the flesh and the devil. The disciples on the road to Emmaus were aware of their hearts being warmed in the company of Jesus by his exposition of the Scriptures. It is as we hear God's Word that we too meet with Jesus in a way that ministers to our situation and need. It was as a result of hearing the Scriptures explained that the two disciples asked so earnestly that Jesus should stay with them, even though they still had not recognized him. When we really want him, he makes himself known to us. The meaning of Jesus appearing 'in a different form' is not clear. To Mary he seemed to be the gardener, and to the two travellers he seemed to be a companion. We are left wondering in what form Jesus appeared to Peter. John 21:1-14 may suggest he seemed a fisherman. Certainly John 21:15-22 makes clear that Jesus was still the same patient, forbearing Master that he had always been.

The unexpected visitor

Read also Luke 24:25-42

The risen Jesus kept on coming to his disciples, all of whom must have been aware of just how deeply they had failed in the time of testing. The table the eleven sat at was, as far as we know, just an ordinary meal-table and not a table of remembrance, such as they had been taught about in the upper room on the night Jesus had been betrayed. It is often in the ordinary things of life that Jesus comes to us. The disciples had not expected him, and some of them thought they were seeing a ghost (Luke 24:36-40). We must note it was their unbelief and hardness of heart that Jesus rebuked, making no mention of how they had run away and how they had failed him in spite of all their teaching and privileges. It is almost as if Jesus was saying to them, as he needs to say to us, 'Don't dwell on your past blunders. I make all things new. Why did you not believe when you were told the glorious truth that I am alive, victorious, and coming to you?' Their unbelief had not only robbed them of their peace and left them full of anxiety; it had stolen from them their hopes and expectations for the future. No doubt they were shattered, unhappy and depressed because of their failure, and in measure that was natural, and they deserved to be unhappy. But over against that were the facts that the Saviour had risen, sin and death had been conquered, and evil had been shown to be powerless in the face of the mighty Son of God. Unbelief is sinful (Heb. 3:12). It hinders, and introduces confusion into the lives of the people of God and his work for them. Unbelief has to be dealt with, and sometimes the Lord allows us to live in the misery of unbelief, until we are ready to listen. That is the story of Thomas in John 20:24-29. We must learn to believe what God says to us in his Word, even if it seems impossible.

The Great Commission

Read also Matthew 28:16-20

When the unbelief of the disciples had been rebuked, and when they realized that Jesus had neither ignored them nor rejected them, but had come to them, then they were in the right frame of mind to receive from him the great gospel commission. It must have astonished and thrilled them to realize that they were still trusted to do the work of God for which they had been prepared. According to Matthew 28:16-20 the scene has changed from Jerusalem to Galilee, which was the place appointed by Jesus for his meeting with them (Matt. 28:6-10). Just exactly when the disciples made the journey to Galilee, and where in Galilee the meeting-place was, and how public or private it was, we are not told. Mark records the commission briefly but with clarity and astonishing depth. The disciples were to preach the good news from God: the account of what God had done for the salvation of sinners in the life, death and resurrection of his Son Jesus Christ. It is a salvation promised and prepared for in the Old Testament, recorded in history in the four Gospels, expounded in its doctrinal and practical fulness in the Epistles of the New Testament, and revealed in its glory and eternal consummation in the Book of Revelation. In a very real sense it is not simple, and yet it is quite plain. The fact is that Jesus Christ came into the world to save sinners (1 Tim. 1:15). The full glory of that statement takes the whole of the Bible to expound and the whole of life to grasp and experience. Note Matthew's emphasis on 'all' and 'always'. The one to whom all power belongs is always with us. We are not on our own and, as we go on in service, we are glad to confess that apart from him we can do nothing (John 15:4-5).

Belief expressed

Read also Luke 12:13-21; 16:19-31

We must not read into this verse that baptism is essential to salvation. That would be to understand the verse in a way that does not conform to the general teaching of Scripture. The real emphasis is on the radical difference between faith and unbelief, and the equally radical consequence of these attitudes. The believer is saved, justified by faith alone (Rom. 5:1), and the unbeliever is condemned. Unbelief is not a weakness, limitation, or misunderstanding. Unbelief is a refusal to believe in spite of all evidences, appeals and warnings. If we go to the great gospel text, John 3:16-18, we find the saving love of God set over against the possibility of perishing. The action of God is declared to be one of saving, not condemning. But the clear statement is made that the unbeliever is condemned already. In the liberal wing of the church, and in society in general, there seems to be a belief in universalism: the idea that all go to heaven in the end. Because of this it is not surprising that there is little emphasis on the need to be saved. Salvation must be set over against the danger of being condemned, excluded from God's presence, and of paying the ultimate spiritual death penalty, which the Bible speaks of as hell. Perhaps in past days there was too much harsh and unfeeling preaching about judgement and hell. But now it seems that the theme of 'Rescue the perishing' has almost been replaced by the emphasis that Jesus will satisfy the heart and solve your problems. It was Jesus who posed the question, 'What shall it profit a man, if he shall gain the whole world, and lose his own soul?' (Mark 8:36, AV). People tend to forget that they have souls that need to be saved. In Luke 12:13-21; 16:19-31 both men were so preoccupied with this life that they forgot to prepare for the life to come.

Test the spirits

Read also Matthew 7:21-23; Revelation 13:11-14

Luke 16:19-31 makes it clear that if people will not hear God's Word when it is preached, then no amount of 'signs and wonders', not even the resurrection, will lead them to believe. We need to understand the limits of the significance of 'signs' before we ponder just what is meant by Mark 16:17-18. We do not deny the miraculous, nor the fact that many astonishing things happened in apostolic times, and still happen. Nor must we ever say that God does not do certain things nowadays. God is free to act in whatever way he chooses, and he has the perfect right to do so. But we must not say that these dramatic, miraculous signs are of the *essence* of the gospel, nor that they must be present if ministry is authentically biblical and spiritual. In actual fact persecutions, imprisonments, suffering and struggling were far more evident in apostolic ministry than miracles were. We must also recognize that in modern times, as in apostolic times and Old Testament times, miracles have been performed by godless unbelievers. Think of Pharaoh's magicians in Exodus 7:10-13,22. Think of the manifestations of evil in the Book of Revelation (Rev. 13:11-14), and of Jesus' words in Matthew 7:21-23; and be careful. Miracles may not be all that significant. They may be a concession to weakness of faith rather than a sign of spirituality. Some of the things spoken of in these verses have been indulged in with disastrous results, and we must recognize that there are people who are susceptible to the unusual, and are vulnerable in the hands of those who manipulate them. Of course God, being kind and caring, reassures and confirms people in their faith in a whole variety of ways and we must not be quick to 'write off' their experiences. Nor must we be quick to copy them.

True signs

Read also 2 Corinthians 12:1-10

Think of these verses in general terms. The powers of evil, however deep-seated, can be cast out of our lives by God, either by swift or slow processes, and a progressive liberation of the whole personality is the result. New tongues can be thought of in terms of speech, which is, of course, an expression of personality. When people begin to speak of new subjects, to speak of God and of spiritual matters, and to speak in a whole new way, then there is every reason to believe that a significant spiritual change has taken place. At the same time it is disturbing when people who claim to be Christians never seem to speak happily and naturally about God. Snakes with deadly bites may be thought of in terms of those things that once tormented our lives but now lose their deadly power. If drinking poison is an act of deliberate bravado that is hard to justify in any sense. Jesus refused when the devil tempted him to do something extraordinary (Matt. 4:5-7). In the matter of miracle cures we must remember that Jesus did not always touch the person, but his word healed. It is the same today. The Word of Jesus spoken, heard and believed, makes men and women whole in a variety of ways, as the person becomes healed in spirit, in mind, in emotions, all to the benefit of the body's health. There is just no limit to what God can do, but he does it in his own perfect ways. Sometimes he heals, sometimes he doesn't. Sometimes deep affliction is left so that spiritual service might be richer and fuller to God's glory (1 Peter 1:3-7).

Christ ascended

Read also Hebrews 4:14-16; 7:24-25; 9:24-28

The fact that Jesus ascended into heaven and took his seat at God's right hand is something we tend to forget, but it is of great importance. Luke, both at the end of his first volume of the story of Jesus and at the beginning of Acts, his second volume, records the historical event (Luke 24:50-53; Acts 1:9-11). The risen Christ, his work completed, his victory manifested, was taken up into heaven. The 'cloud' referred to in Acts, which received Jesus out of their sight, would signify for all Jews the presence and the glory of God (Exod. 16:10; Matt. 17:5). As Jesus parted from his disciples his hands were raised in blessing. Perhaps he spoke the familiar words of the Aaronic blessing in Numbers 6:22-26. Mark simply says that Jesus sat down at the right hand of God, emphasizing his lordship. In every sense, Jesus is Lord: Lord of our lives and circumstances; Lord over the powers of men and devils; Lord over the course of history and of the whole of God's plan of salvation. It was an awareness of the lordship of Christ that caused Paul to testify that the things that had happened to him, which at first seemed disastrous, had in fact resulted in the furtherance of the gospel (Phil. 1:12; Rom. 8:28). When we pray to be used in the service of the gospel, our prayers are answered in the wisdom of the one who is Lord of all. Whatever our work, our situation, our battles, failures and successes, we are never on our own. Read Hebrews 4:14-16; 7:25; 9:24 and think of both the immediate and the long-lasting impact of this on the disciples. Every time they thought of the risen Saviour they would think of him as the great High Priest, looking upon them, blessing them, and appearing in the very presence of God on their behalf. We all tend to forget what a great intercessor we have.

Into the future

Read also Acts 2:32-36; Ephesians 1:18-22

The fact that Jesus is ascended into heaven is the ground of our confidence and hope. He sat down, because his work was finished. Sin was dealt with, salvation secured and the issues settled (Heb. 1:1-3). The practical outworking of the victory and lordship of Jesus is fulfilled in our lives and service by the power of the Holy Spirit (Acts 2:33). That was the enabling power of the apostles as they went forward in obedience to their great commission. When we read that the disciples went out and preached, we must remember that they did so under orders (v. 15). This is one of the basic elements in all Christian service. We must know that we are doing what God has commanded us to do. The Lord is King, and he is head over all in the interest of the church (Eph. 1:22). In all our work in the service of the gospel, we are personally supervised and directed by the one whose wisdom and power are perfect. In every sense the government is on his shoulders, and it is by his energy that the work is accomplished (Isa. 9:6-7). There is something gloriously thrilling and reassuring in the statement that the Lord worked with them and confirmed the message. We must never forget the unceasing, unfettered working of God the Holy Spirit through the Word of God as it is being preached. The sword that the Spirit uses is the Word (Eph. 6:17) and God has total confidence in his Word, which accomplishes what it is sent to do (Isa. 55:8-11). When God's servants are very aware of their weaknesses and limitations, they are reassured that God himself watches over his Word to perform it (Jer. 1:12, AV).

God at work

Read also Romans 10:8-17

Mark emphasizes that they preached, and preaching is the means by which the work of the gospel goes forward. But what is preaching? It is reasoning out of the Scriptures, setting forth the person and work of Christ (Acts 17:2-3; 18:4). It is the open statement of the truth of God by those who recognize that it *is* God's truth and therefore not to be tampered with (2 Cor. 4:1-2). An essential element in preaching God's Word is to make sure that the person of the preacher, his personality and his gifts, do not get in the way (2 Cor. 4:5,7). The 'signs' that confirmed the message must not be thought of simply in terms of miraculous signs. Seed growing to fruitfulness, and lives being built in spiritual and moral integrity are the ultimate signs. Sometimes God allows us to see what he is doing in order to encourage us. At other times he simply asks us to trust him and to go on. Because Jesus is Lord there is no doubt about the final issue. Neither is there doubt or confusion about the processes by which the final victory is brought to pass. This was something the early apostles thrilled to as they went forward in their God-given work. Read Acts 2:32-36; 7:54-56; Ephesians 1:18-22; Philippians 2:9-11; Hebrews 10:12-14 and 1 Corinthians 15:24-25. Jesus is Lord, and with him we go into the future with confidence.